You Must Be My Best Friend ...

Because I Hate You!

You Must Be My Best Friend ...
Because I Hate You

Friendship
and How to Survive It

Emily Dubberley

f

First published in 2005 by Fusion Press,
a division of Satin Publications Ltd.
101 Southwark Street
London SE1 0JF
UK
info@visionpaperbacks.co.uk
www.visionpaperbacks.co.uk
Publisher: Sheena Dewan

© Emily Dubberley 2005

The right of Emily Dubberley to be identified as the author of the work has been asserted by her in accordance with the Copyright, Designs and Patents Act of 1988.

All rights reserved. No part of this publication may be reproduced, stored in a retrieval system, or transmitted in any form or by any means, electronic, mechanical, photocopying, recording or otherwise, without prior written permission of the publisher.

A catalogue record for this book is available from the British Library.

ISBN: 1-904132-76-6

2 4 6 8 10 9 7 5 3 1

Cover photo: Getty Images/The Image Bank
Cover and text design by ok?design
Printed and bound in the UK by Mackays of Chatham Ltd,
Chatham, Kent

To single out just one friend would mean everyone else would hate me, and there's no way I'm risking that. So, to all my friends, past, present and future, thanks for everything you've taught me, and all the fun we've had.

Contents

Acknowledgements		ix
Introduction		1
Chapter 1:	Friendship: The Basics	5
Chapter 2:	The Life Cycle of Friendships	59
Chapter 3:	Unequal Friendships	109
Chapter 4:	When Friends Collide	133
Chapter 5:	Sex and Friendship	151
Chapter 6:	In It for the Long Haul	189
Conclusion:	Friends till the End	233
Useful Resources		239
About the Author		241

Acknowledgements

Thanks to:

All the friends who've helped me on this book directly or indirectly; whether through reading drafts of this through for me, telling me their friendship stories and asking everyone they knew to share their stories as well (the joy of email), buying me cigarettes and cava when I was too immersed in writing to leave my computer, turning up with food and cold-cures when I was laid up in bed so I'd get better quicker, dragging me out to dance when I was getting cabin fever, or steam-cleaning my carpets when I got distracted because my flat was a tip. You all rock.

In particular, thanks to Simon Batistoni, Joe Bidgood, Steve Boardman, Anne Cantelo, Paul Carr, Monique Carty, Christina Carty, Avril Cooper, Elizabeth Easther, Julia Gash, The Girl, Caroline Gold, John Handelaar, Sarah Hedley, Margret Hotze, Steve Lamacq, Sarah Lewis, Bibi Lynch, Beth McLoughlin, Mark Meeson, Mil Millington, Marcelle Perks, Alex Rees, Michael Smith, Devan Willemberg, Simon Wistow and Chrissie

You Must Be My Best Friend ...

Wright. And yes, that's deliberately in alphabetical order so I don't get into a load of friendship conflict because people think they're less important to me than other people I've mentioned first. You think I learned nothing from writing this book?

My family, in particular Jean Dubberley and Juliet Dubberley (or my mum and sister as I know them, but it's way cooler if you get your full name in a book).

My psychology tutors, particularly Dennis Howitt, for getting me so enthused about the way that people work.

And my agent Chelsey Fox, along with everyone at Fusion Press, particularly publicity queen, Emily Bird, genius editor, Charlotte Cole and wonderful sub, Louise Coe — thanks for not only being so ace with my first book, and getting this one out there so quickly afterwards, but for also turning into people I consider more friends than colleagues.

Introduction

Most books on friendship are saccharine tomes about how wonderful friends are; they make life easier, are the new family and will 'be there for you when the rain starts to pour', as the TV series claimed. But that only gives one side of the story.

OK, so friendship is fab, and most of us would hate the idea of being without our pals, but it's a myth that having a circle of good friends is an *easy* way to enhance your life. Real friendship takes work, and can drive you up the wall. Sometimes, your best friend will call to have a moaning session about the idiot bloke she's dating and you'll think, 'Well, if you'd listened to my advice the last 30 times we had this conversation you wouldn't be in the situation you're in …' At other times, you'll be the one needing support and all that your best friend is able to witter on about is her new job/man/hobby. Managing expectations, and making sure that you have a balanced relationship with your pals, takes time and effort.

You Must Be My Best Friend ...

Friends can gossip, hurt your feelings, get depressed, develop addictions that you could do without, fall in with people who are bad news — and, sometimes, your friends will just be plain old boring. But no one dares admit that friendship is about anything more than a loving support network that gives you a warm feeling inside, or tells you how to deal with problems that you're bound to encounter. While there are endless books out there on relationships, when was the last time you saw a book called 'Getting Over Her: What to Do When Your Best Friend Ditches You'?

Friendship gets even tougher to negotiate the closer you get to each other. You might face the joys of holidaying with a pal, only to discover that, while your idea of heaven is ogling Miguel the waiter and lazing by the pool, she wants to get up at 7am to go and check out some crusty old ruin (no, not Miguel's dad). Many a friendship has ended because of too many Pina Coladas in the sun.

And then there's living with a friend. It may seem like a good idea when you live apart from each other, get your telephone bill through and realise that you've spent hundreds of pounds chatting to your best friend over the last month. 'Surely it'd be more practical to live together than spend all this money talking on the phone,' you think. But a hefty phone bill is a small price to pay compared to falling out with someone you care about. And no matter how close you may be to start with, it's much easier to like someone when they haven't finished your milk for the third time in a week, and put the empty carton

Introduction

back into the fridge; or kept you awake all night by shagging the barman from your local so loudly you felt like you were involved in a threesome; or left their bright purple top in the washing machine meaning you inadvertently turn your entire white wash mauve.

This book busts the myth that friendship is all nights giggling over cocktails and snuggly slumber parties. It looks at all the common friendship dilemmas no one talks about: 'third-wheel' syndrome — when you get a new best friend, introduce her to the woman who's been your best friend for years and things go horribly wrong (or your pal does the same thing to you); sex and friendship — from fancying your friend (male or female — bicuriosity has certainly added a new load of complications to friendship) to dealing with it when their new partner (or worse, long-term lover) comes on to you; jealousy in all its forms; what to do when you outgrow a relationship; maintaining a friendship when your lifestyles or locations change; and every kind of 'bad friend' act you could possibly imagine.

If you have friends, and want to keep them (or dump them), you need to read this book.

Chapter One

Friendship: The Basics

Do you remember how friendship worked when you were at school: tentatively deciding who to sit next to, because the choice you made would decide which social group you belonged to; picking teams during games lessons – or standing there hoping desperately that your friend who was picking teams didn't leave you until last marking you out as a social pariah; having rows that ended with 'we're not friends any more'; and much hair-flicking and storming off to hang out with another group of friends who you instructed, 'Don't talk to *her*'? Think things have moved on since then? Think again.

OK, it's unlikely that you'll sulk for a week because your best friend borrowed your favourite Barbie pen and chewed the end (probably). But replace the Barbie pen with your new designer shoes and the chewing with scuffing, and you'll see how little things have changed since you were a kid.

Most people have had to juggle a party guest list because one friend inadvertently ended up dating another one's ex-boyfriend

You Must Be My Best Friend ...

and you know they'll come to blows if they're in the same space; have been double-booked on a Saturday night and had to choose which friend to see; or have spent a day shopping with a friend, only to realise that, actually, said person is seriously dull when you have to spend five hours with them.

Many friendships have faltered in the face of a holiday together or, worse, flat-sharing. And while you may not actively tell your friends 'don't talk to her', if another friend gets on your wrong side, let's face it, if some girl's just stolen your bloke leaving you broken-hearted and sobbing, there's an unwritten 'girlie code' that says only a rubbish pal of yours would continue to chat to her.

Over a lifetime, the average person makes 396 friends, but of those they only stay in touch with 33; that's one in twelve — a situation that over two-thirds (68 per cent) call one of their 'biggest regrets in life'. Someone you feel incredibly close to at one stage in your life could be little more than an acquaintance — or even a stranger — a few years later. Conversely, friendships that start off as casual, with the occasional beer here and party invitation there, can get closer over time.

According to a survey by MSN Messenger, most people have 33 friends at any one time, but the majority of these are seen as 'social friends'. Somewhat scarily, of all the hundreds of pals you make over the years, most of us only have six people that we'd consider true friends at any one time. Obviously, surveys are based on averages, so don't panic if you've got less pals than that (or feel smug if you've got more). After all, do you really want to be average? Added to which, friendships vary over the course of your life, so even if you've only got one close pal at the moment, it doesn't mean that will always be the case.

Anne's story: Friendships change over time

> In my experience there are two types of friends: 'Social' friends and 'soul' friends. Social friends are the people you hang out with every day because you live near each other, share lifestyles and enjoy each other's company. Soul friends are those you keep in contact with whatever happens in your life. Social friends may become soul friends, but only a change in circumstance will tell you that. When you get married, when you have children and when you separate, social friends will disappear; the ones that are left are soul friends.

In a strange twist, we tend to see our social friends more frequently than our true friends. Women see their social friends on average every three-and-a-half days, and men see theirs an average of once every five days: but both genders meet up with their close friends once every eight weeks. So maybe there's some truth in the saying 'absence makes the heart grow fonder'.

This research also suggests that we have different needs for different friends. Humans are social animals, and need company – but just because a friend sees other people more often than

You Must Be My Best Friend ...

they see you, it doesn't mean that you're a 'lesser' friend. It could be that they only want to see you when they've got time and energy to devote to you, while the other people they see are there purely to gossip to about nothing important, after a hard day's work. Just because you don't see a pal for a while, it doesn't mean that there's no deep connection.

In fact, according to Jan Yager, author of *Who's That Sitting At My Desk?*, it takes an average of three years to know whether or not someone is a true friend. So it's pretty obvious that real friendship is as much about coping with the long haul — earning a person's trust and learning to trust them — as it is about having frivolous times together. Partying and shopping together can be a damned good way to spend time while you're getting to know each other, but it's when the shit hits the fan that friendships really start to deepen.

Friends are often the most important people in our lives. At any one time, about half of the UK population and around a third of the US population are single, meaning that we rely on friends for emotional and practical support. Sure, some people have a close family they can rely on in emergencies, but most of us tend to turn to our pals in times of crisis; think of all those wine-soaked 'why hasn't he called?' phone-calls, the hours of bitching about the boss who's just made you redundant from the job of your dreams, and staying on a friend's floor when you can't afford to pay rent because you've just lost said job.

Yes, friends offer an essential support network. But if your best pal suddenly dumps you because of a misunderstanding or

Friendship: The Basics

conflict, there's no coping mechanism in place. She (or he) is the person you'd normally turn to; without them around, you have to fall back on 'lesser' friends. And you'll get much less sympathy for being ditched by a friend than you will for being dumped by a sexual partner – even if the friendship has lasted ten years to the relationship's ten weeks.

Negotiating your way through friendships can be tricky. With sexual relationships, there's a natural expectation that you'll both have to compromise. With friendships, it's much easier to end up in negative patterns without realising it; one of you always picks the restaurants you go to, or is the person who calls to arrange meeting up. We put up with behaviour from friends that we'd find utterly unacceptable in a relationship, giving them the benefit of the doubt, or sitting on problems hoping that they'll blow over. We suffer friendships that are long past their sell-by date, because, well, it's only friendship, and saying, 'I don't want to be friends with you any more,' seems melodramatic, or at the very least, a bit 'eight-year-old'. We even put up with friends who are seriously toxic, for fear of being perceived as oversensitive if we pull them up on their behaviour.

Conversely, we have higher expectations of friendship than of relationships; after all, there are endless articles about the myriad reasons that a partner might let you down (most of which get oversimplified to 'because men are crap' – which may be unfair, but, hell, that's the world we're living in). Friendship, on the other hand, is expected to be flawless: if you believe the media, a friend is someone who should make you laugh, ensure you get home safely when you've had one too many cocktails, defend you in an argument, go shopping with you, listen to your worries and be responsible for your social life. That's quite a demand to put on anyone.

Yes, friendship is complicated. But before racing ahead to dealing with all the dilemmas it's worth taking a look at the various kinds of friend that are out there.

FRIENDSHIP CATEGORIES

Best friends

The ultimate pal to have, a best friend is the one you feel closer to than almost anyone else. Research by Queendom.com shows that 39 per cent of women and 20 per cent of men turn to their best friend first if they have a crisis. You might find it disturbing to know that 28 per cent of women have sexual fantasies about their male best friend, and 38 per cent of men fantasise about their female best friend; or that a further 28 per cent of women and 17 per cent of men fantasise about their same-sex best friend. But sexual kicks aren't what best-friendship is about. A best friend is someone who 'gets' you — often in the same kind of way that a partner does. They have your best interests at heart (well, unless you're both going after the same dress in a sale, or man in a dry spell) and you never need a reason to call them. You can be yourself in front of your best friend,

Friendship: The Basics

without them thinking that you're mad/gross/boring. (Well, mostly anyway: picking your nose and eating it isn't something that should ever be done, even in front of your best friend. What are you, five?)

Some best-friendships are formed during childhood and you've always stayed in contact; others are created during adulthood. Sometimes it can be a whirlwind thing, where you meet each other and bond instantly. At other times, you can know each other vaguely for years and it's only when a particular situation arises — say, one of you facing a crisis, or the pair of you ending up working together so that you spend much more time together — that the friendship moves up a level. But however it starts, one thing's for sure: your best friend is the one you'd miss the most if he or she wasn't around.

Tracey's story: I started off hating my best friend

Emma and I first met at university. She was editor of the student newspaper and I was one of their writers. We never got on all that well, but she suggested that I stood in the student election to take over as newspaper editor when she finished her year, because I spent all my time in the office and was one of her most reliable writers.

I won the election, and she started training me for the job. From day one there was friction: I felt intimidated by her

You Must Be My Best Friend ...

because everyone said she was the best editor ever, and, I later found out, she felt similarly uncomfortable because I was taking over 'her baby'. It would be safe to say that the experience didn't exactly make us close. We bickered constantly and I often ended up crying myself to sleep when I got home. That said, the training she gave me was brilliant and I really respected her for her initial help as my year as editor progressed. But we didn't really chat at all – we just got on with our own lives.

Fast-forward a year and I was graduating: she still had a year of her course to finish. I moved to the city to work but still popped back to university for occasional events. On one such occasion, we bumped into each other and made small talk, as you do. She mentioned that she had an interview near where I lived, and I – being somewhat tipsy – said she could sleep on my sofa if she needed somewhere to stay. In hindsight, neither of us is sure why I asked, or why she said yes – she had other friends she could have stayed with – but we're both glad that she did.

The night that she stayed over, we ended up chatting for hours. We discovered endless common ground we hadn't ever noticed was there and realised that our initial dislike of each other was down to mutual insecurity. Not only were we both attached to the newspaper we edited but I'd thought that she'd spread various rumours about me, and, as it happened, she'd thought the same thing about me. Neither of us was right. We spent the evening clearing the air and by the time morning rolled around, we knew that we'd got the basis of a firm friendship.

Friendship: The Basics

As luck would have it, she got the job and ended up moving in with me. We dated a couple of men who were best mates* so we ended up spending almost every hour with each other. When, years later, I split up with a long-term boyfriend, she was the one who offered me her spare room, and hours of support. When she had a serious medical problem, I was the one that she turned to.

Ten years on, we're still the best of friends. I'd never judge on first impressions again – if I'd stuck with my original assessment, I'd have missed out on getting to know someone who's now an essential part of my life.

Childhood friends

Some people stay in contact with friends from their youth, others don't. On the one hand, it can be great having someone around who has so much common ground; who knows what your mum's like when she's on the warpath, snuck into the same bars as you did when you were too young to drink and compared notes on that first kiss at the time it first happened. On the other hand, it can be tricky to get out of childhood roles. If you were always the geeky one and your friend was the popular one, this can stick into adulthood, even if you're nothing like the person you were as a kid. Common ground is all very well, but only if you can both accept that the person

* ***A note for US readers***: In the UK, 'mate' means buddy, so don't panic – they weren't getting it on!

you knew as a child may not exist any more, as change is a natural part of growing up. Otherwise, one of you may end up holding the other one back in life.

Tammi's story: She couldn't move on

Billie was my best mate when I was four. Even though she was the year above me at school, we went everywhere together and I was honoured to be the only person outside her classmates who was allowed at her birthday parties. When we got to 11, we ended up going to different schools and drifted apart. I didn't think about her, other than if I found an old school picture, but when she called me about 20 years later, having seen my name on Friends Reunited, I was pleased to hear from her and we arranged to meet up for a drink.

When she arrived, we got on well enough, but I realised that our lives were very different now. I'd moved from our hometown, she hadn't; I was very career-focused, she worked for her mum in a job she wasn't that interested in. But when she said she'd brought a stack of old school pictures with her, I thought it would be fun to look through them with her for old times' sake.

She got a picture album out and I was horrified to hear her running commentary as she progressed through the book. She knew what every single person in the pictures was doing now: whether they were single or attached, whereabouts they lived

Friendship: The Basics

– even if they'd ever had a run-in with the police. Bearing in mind that there were about 30 kids in her class and the pictures had been taken 20 years previously, I was disturbed. When I found out that she still had a crush on the same boy that she'd fancied at school – even though he'd subsequently come out and was living with his boyfriend – I realised that this was a woman who truly did find her schooldays the happiest of her life and was looking to recreate them. I, on the other hand, was entirely happy with my adult life, and the idea of returning to school wasn't my idea of fun. Needless to say, we didn't see each other again.

Work mates

We spend a third of our life at work, so it's not that surprising that we tend to bond with some people there. And while bosses frequently have an issue with people having relationships with colleagues, research from the American Society for Public Administration shows that the benefits of office friendships outweigh the negatives by a factor of four to one. The biggest 'cons' according to employers are increased gossip, office romances (when 'just good friends' isn't enough any more) and distractions from work-related activities. Well, how else are you supposed to spend your time in the office – actually doing your job?

When it comes to work mates, it could be that your only common ground is a mutual loathing of the boss, or it could

You Must Be My Best Friend ...

be that you'd stay friends even if one of you left the company. You can generally tell if the latter's the case if you end up seeing each other at weekends as well as work nights, or find yourself wanting to call your work mate when you have some life dilemma, or a piece of good news that's unrelated to your job.

Of all the types of friendship, this is the one most likely to have to cope with external conflict: say, you get promoted and your friend doesn't; or you don't see eye to eye on a work issue, which has a knock-on effect to the way you perceive each other out of work. Work friendships can be risky too. If you misread the strength of a friendship, you may find that your 'outside work' confessions about what really happened with the new guy at the office party get back to your boss, or your admission that as a teenager you experimented with drugs soon becomes office rumour and adversely affects your career. Even if your work friend wasn't the one who breached your confidence, this situation can put doubt in your mind and make you lose faith in her, sometimes both professionally and personally.

According to sociologist and author Jan Yager, the seven major things that you should never discuss with work mates are business confidences that would violate trust or ethics if shared, family secrets that could put a family member in jeopardy, sexual affairs (either ongoing or past), sexual comments about your other half, anything you wouldn't feel happy about having repeated in a national newspaper, politically incorrect

Friendship: The Basics

views and any negative feelings about clients or people you work with. But if you rule that lot out, there's not a lot of scope for gossip left – and it's a pretty dull basis for friendship.

Instead, as a general rule, if you both protect each other's confidences and have a strong line that neither of you cross, taking care to ensure your friendship doesn't impact on your career, and vice versa, it is very possible that a work friendship can be one of the closest friendships that you have, other than with your best friend. After all, you're spending a huge amount of time together, and, chances are, you're relatively similar individuals if you've both been drawn to work in the same kind of environment.

Jemma's story: Work brought us together

Lucy and I had known of each other for years – we both work in media and it's quite a small world. However, we didn't have any direct contact with each other until someone sent a vitriolic letter about her into my newspaper. It was full of spurious allegations and quite clearly written by someone who was unhinged. I emailed her to let her know, saying that there was no way that I'd print it but I thought she should know what this person was saying. It turned out that it was someone deliberately running a smear campaign against her. She offered to take me out for a drink to say thanks for letting her know, and we ended up bonding over many glasses of wine.

You Must Be My Best Friend ...

We said we should do it again soon, but our work schedules were so busy that we somehow never got the time.

About a year later, I was offered a job at a new publication and was looking for staff. She sprang to mind instantly, but I didn't think she'd go for it as it was a new project that would involve a lot of risk and she had a secure job at the time. However, we met up to discuss it and I was overjoyed when she said she'd take it.

The nature of the job meant that we spoke to each other every day and were frequently on the phone to each other into the early hours. Soon, I was in contact with her more often than I spoke to my best friend. Over many months, and many late night meetings in the pub, it became obvious that we'd got more and more in common. At one point, things were going really badly in my life, and I called her to offload. She spent hours listening to me (even when I was crying and she could barely make out what I was saying). That was the point at which I realised quite how important she'd become to me. When she called me about her own life problems a while later, I realised that it was a two-way street – we were no longer people who worked together, but had a real friendship.

Now, I count Lucy as one of my best friends. Working with her is a joy – coming up with ideas for the newspaper is more like a couple of mates talking about their life than actual work. She's one of the first people I turn to if something important happens in my life, and I've trusted her with some of my darkest secrets.

I've recently been looking at moving to another job but I know, whether we work together or not, Lucy is someone that I love having in my life and would hate to be without. There's no way I could ever see her as just a colleague now.

Fun friends

Not all friendships are based on a deep emotional connection. A fun friend is the person you find yourself partying with on a regular basis, but somehow never see unless there's something else going on in the background to entertain you. Drinking, dancing and frivolity abound whenever you're together but remove the intoxicants and you probably don't have an awful lot in common. Still, it's good to be with someone who knows the dance routine to Madonna's 'Vogue' just as well as you. And while she may not be the best person to turn to for a shoulder to cry on when the love of your life dumps you, she's the perfect friend to take you out on the pull and help you get over him by getting under someone else, once you've wiped away your tears.

Serena's story: Dancing queen

I met Jennie one night in a club. We were both drunk and got chatting to each other at the bar. We'd both lost the friends we'd come with (both of them had pulled, leaving us alone)

You Must Be My Best Friend ...

so, when it turned out that we lived in the same direction, we decided to share a cab back together. She was a really good laugh and we ended up swapping numbers. When she called me the following week to see if I was going to the club again, I arranged to meet her there.

When we first saw each other, conversation was stilted, but after a few drinks, we were dancing with each other and giggling like old friends. She was a natural at getting us talking with fit men on the dance floor, and I had a fantastic night out.

We arranged to meet up and get ready together the following week. Again, conversation didn't really flow at first but as the night progressed, we started having fun.

I didn't really notice there was any problem with this until we decided to go shopping together. It became very obvious that, other than the club, we had very little to talk about. She didn't seem to notice though, and I thought I was just judging her too harshly, because it was rapidly becoming clear that she wasn't as intelligent as me.

Since then, we've met up at the club on a regular basis, and gone out for coffee a couple of times, but we've never really bonded: her interests seem to be make-up, celebrities and the latest fashion, whereas I prefer talking about books or philosophy or, well, anything that requires a brain. That said, I do love clubbing with her because she's the ultimate party animal.

Now, any time she suggests meeting up outside the club, I find myself making excuses. She's a really nice person but

Friendship: The Basics

I don't want to invest any more time in developing the friendship as it's clear that, partying aside, there's nothing going on.

Useful friends

Though this category can overlap with others, and is less common than the others, some people — particularly those who are very career-minded — have friends who are more for what they can provide than because of any particular emotional connection. This could be a network of contacts, a perfect eye for fashion or a car. Often, there's a mutual dependency: say, you know all the best networking events to go to and can get your 'useful friend' in there for free — and she just happens to have a gorgeous flat in a convenient location that you can crash in after your night out.

The biggest challenge with this kind of friendship is making sure that you keep an eye on the balance of it: you don't want to be a sponger, or conversely, get taken for granted. But as long as you're both using each other, there's nothing wrong.

One word of warning though: do bear in mind that a 'useful friend' is probably not the kind of person you'd want to call when your world implodes. Unless, of course, the reason she's useful is that she knows people who can help put your life back together again.

You Must Be My Best Friend ...

Suni's story: We swap contacts

I met Gina through work at a networking event. She's involved in the corporate side of business, whereas I'm in marketing. We got on well when we first met and it soon became apparent that we worked with a lot of complementary people. We fell into a routine of meeting up to exchange leads: she'd tell me who'd got budget coming up and I'd tell her the angle to pitch her clients to the press with.

We would meet up with each other at least once a week – we even ended up spending a Christmas together once, when both of us were too busy to take a proper break because of work – but, if I'm honest, the relationship is more about our contacts than anything else. There's nothing wrong with her – she's just at a different life stage to me. She's still single and wants to go out to find men, whereas I'm married and have just had a baby. I could imagine nothing worse than going to a loud and trashy nightclub, getting drunk and crawling home with some stranger, and that's pretty much her whole life outside work.

I'm sure she finds me as boring as I find her, but we still keep in contact because it's just too useful professionally. Sometimes I feel like I'm taking advantage, but she gets as much out of it as I do. I just wish that we got on as well socially as we do professionally so I didn't feel like such a bitch.

Friendship: The Basics

'In case of emergency' friends

Not a friend that you call when things go pear-shaped (that's a role for the best mate), these are the pals you have on the sexual back-burner in case you're ever so desperate to have a relationship that you decide to 'settle'. Think marriage pacts ('If we're both single when we're 40, let's get hitched — I mean, we've got enough in common.') or drunken fumbles when you're horny as hell.

Sometimes these friends are exes, sometimes they're people you've never quite got round to getting it on with because you don't fancy them quite enough and sometimes they're 'might-have-beens', where the timing has never quite seemed right. Whatever the case, you have to guard against this kind of friendship being too one-sided: if one of you is secretly pining for the other, things can end in tears. If they're the one who's desperate to hook up with you, do the decent thing and let your poor mate down gently. And if it's you that's keener, just let it go. It will probably never happen. After all, if you think about it, how many people do you know who really *do* end up marrying one of their friends because of a marriage pact? And if the attraction is one-sided, you'll never have a successful relationship anyway.

Greta's story: He's on the back burner

I've known Chris for years. He hangs out with the same friendship circle as I do, and there's always been a bit of a frisson between us. However, timing-wise things have never worked out and now we've known each other for too long for things to progress romantically.

Nonetheless, every time we go out, we end up flirting. More worryingly, I've noticed that he moves up my friendship list whenever I'm single. I'm usually fine with only seeing him once or twice every couple of months, and chatting sporadically, but every time I get dumped, I'm on the phone to him for hours at a time and tend to see him much more. It's great to get the ego boost from him, because he's so flirtatious, even though I know that nothing will ever happen. I guess that he feels the same way, because I tend to hear from him a lot more when he's not getting any action.

We've had long conversations about what we'd do if we were both single when we were 30 and even jokingly agreed that, because we get on so well, we should get married if we didn't meet anyone else by then. But deep down, I know that he's only a security blanket. It's just that sometimes, I really wouldn't mind getting under him.

* * *

No matter what kind of friendship you have, it's important that you keep your expectations realistic. Some people assume that a friend is someone who devotes every hour to making them happy and seem unaware that it's a two-way process. Others lie back and get walked all over by their friends, while apologising that they haven't written 'doormat' in legible

Friendship: The Basics

enough lettering on their stomach. So are your expectations of friendship reasonable? In the time-honoured fashion, this quiz should help you work it out.

QUIZ

DO YOU EXPECT TOO MUCH FROM YOUR FRIENDS?

1. You've just been dumped by a man that you've been seeing for a few weeks and you're feeling insecure. Your best friend has a hot date with someone she's been trying to land for months. Should she:
   a) Cancel the date and come round with ice cream and tissues?
   b) Spend some time on the phone to you and arrange to meet up for a proper chat the next day?
   c) Wait until after her date to return your call – she should put her own needs first?
   d) Ignore what you're going through – it's not her problem? Anyway, you know from experience that if you do try to chat about it, she'll end up talking more about herself and how your problem relates to her life, than giving you a shoulder to cry on.

2. A promotion has come up at work, and it's your dream job. A friend at work also wants the promotion, though it's less about the job and more about the money to her. Should she:

You Must Be My Best Friend ...

a) Not apply – you're much more suited to the job anyway?
b) Chat to you about it, and agree that the best woman will win?
c) Go for the job without mentioning it to you – it's none of your business?
d) Pick your brains about why you'd be perfect for the job then use your lines in her interview? Every woman for herself.

3. You spot a cute guy when you're out with a mate. She spots him at the same time. Should she:
   a) Let you have him?
   b) Toss a coin with you to see who gets to make the approach – with the understanding that if the first person fails, the other one then has free rein to go for it?
   c) Go for it just as much as you, but without belittling you?
   d) Approach him and explain that you fancy him but are best avoided because of your flaws, listing them all and using them as a way to prove she's better than you?

4. You've just moved in with a friend and the flat is in need of serious redecoration. Should you:
   a) Decorate your room, with her help? You'll do hers after you've decorated all the communal areas but there's no way you can sleep in a hellhole.

Friendship: The Basics

b) Decorate all communal areas together, then each start on your own rooms, pitching in with each other if you get the chance?

c) Decorate her room first together, then do all the communal areas? You can cope with your room being a bit rough to start with — the important thing is that you're living together.

d) Decorate the whole place yourself — she doesn't have time?

If you picked mostly As, you expect too much: friendship is about sharing, not about getting your own way all the time. Lighten up, and remember to give as much as you take.

If you picked mostly Bs, you have a balanced approach to friendship and can see the give and take required to make it work.

If you picked mostly Cs, you're letting yourself get walked all over: you don't have to cave in to someone else's demands to make them like you. A good friend will like you on your own merits, not because you let them get their own way all the time. Stand up for yourself and you'll find your friendships get more balanced.

And if you picked mostly Ds, you have major insecurity issues — there's no way a friend should treat you like this. Hell, even an enemy would deserve a slap for behaving in such a nasty way, as the story below shows.

You Must Be My Best Friend ...

Alexandra's story: She pulls stunts on me

I was probably ten years old, or maybe a bit younger, when my friend Viivi invited me to come with her and her family to their summer cabin by the lake. It was really a big deal for me, since she was the most popular girl in our school and her parents were rich. Besides, she had spent her time mostly with other kids, although I was her oldest friend. So, the day came and she told me they would come and pick me up around 2 o'clock. I walked around all day with a backpack full of all kinds of stuff one needs when one's ten years old and is planning to spend a fun day at the beach.

Well, it wasn't until 5 o'clock when I started to get suspicious and then I called her cell phone (can you even believe that she had one?! I mean, this was 1995 or something and she was a kid!). It turned out that they had gone to the cabin without me. The explanation was that their car was full and she had been too busy to call me (she was sunbathing when I called). As a result my dad got furious and drove me to the cabin himself as I cried, feeling oh so small.

Nowadays Viivi is still the one I'd call my best (and maybe only) friend, although she has pulled some stunts on me. She's been sleeping with guys twice her age since she was 12 and doesn't seem to get that none of them love her. There's one especially tricky case who's been after her for ages (ten years I think, and we're both only 20 at the moment), but he has always dated some other woman and even has a child. These days the

Friendship: The Basics

guy 'falls in love' once a month, but never with Viivi. Viivi starts heavy, uncontrollable drinking every time that happens and swears to me that she'll never see that scumbag again. I'm always, 'That's the spirit, just remember how he is the next time he calls and don't answer!' You can guess whether she takes my advice or not ...

Viivi has even attacked me once because of this guy; it all started with her telling him that I'd said he'd got a nice ass. I don't know why she said that, since I really resent the man, but anyway he replied to her by saying that my ass was quite lovely too. Viivi nearly exploded, and of course this was all my fault. That was somewhat disturbing, but ... she's my best friend and luckily she forgave me.

What is friendship?
Essential guidelines for being a good friend

Of course, friendship is very rarely black and white. Everyone wants different things in a friend — one woman's trivial gossip-queen is another's top trend-setting pal. And while one person's idea of heaven could be someone they can talk to for hours while setting the world to rights, another could think of no worse navel-gazing hell. But, interests aside, there are core attributes that are pretty much universal when it comes to friendship. The top ten things that people look for in a friend are:

You Must Be My Best Friend ...

1. Honesty
2. Trust
3. Loyalty
4. Sense of humour
5. Compassion
6. Fun
7. Love
8. Understanding
9. A good listener
10. Kindness

So, as long as you don't nick your mate's wallet, pretend you didn't do it and give all the cash from it to her mortal enemy, you're already scoring pretty highly as a friend. But, to be serious (kind of), bearing all of those points in mind with your friends is important.

Honest, you look great in purple and lime green Lycra

Honesty may seem like a basic requirement, but can be much harder to achieve in reality. OK, so you don't want a friend who's going to sneak off with your man behind your back (or in front of it!) and you don't want to have to check your wallet every time you go out with a friend in case they've nicked your money. But those are such basic requirements from any reasonable human being that they shouldn't really be a deter-

Friendship: The Basics

mining factor in whether you're friends with someone. They should be taken as read as the right way to behave.

Lady's story: She took my stuff

After a breakup with a boyfriend a few years ago I was invited to go on a last-minute work holiday to Barbados with some colleagues. A girlfriend of mine, not part of my work circle, invited herself along – we were to share a room.

Arriving at the villa we went to the bedroom and I asked Denise which bed she wanted – she said the left one and she went off to find the bathroom. I stayed in the bedroom and noticed that luckily for me Denise had chosen the bed with the dodgy pillow (a skanky sofa cushion crammed into a pillowcase), whereas I had a nice fluffy pillow.

On going to bed after Denise, I found my bed had suddenly acquired said crap pillow and Denise looked very comfy fast asleep with mine – I swapped them back the next day but, alas, it was a homing pillow and mysteriously stayed with me the entire holiday.

She also behaved appallingly in front of my colleagues – cadging drinks and nicking food off people's plates yet never actually buying a round of drinks or even paying for her own meals.

After the holiday unpacking at home I noticed a pair of gold earrings (fairly valuable) were missing from my jewellery bag. I

You Must Be My Best Friend ...

rang Denise to ask if she'd packed them by accident, and my ex-boyfriend answered the phone and passed it over to her (I pretended I didn't realise who had answered and didn't mention it – I was over him already anyway!). She reacted to my simple request about the missing earrings with, 'No, I haven't seen them – have YOU seen my Lou Reed tape?' in the most accusatory fashion (it was a very cheap home-made audio tape!). I concluded that she must have stolen my earrings and never had anything more to do with her from that day on. What a prize bitch!

However, if your favourite dress makes your bum look like an elephant's, would you really want your best friend to tell you, or would you prefer a gentler approach? Similarly, if your best friend's partner comes on to you and tells you that you are much sexier/more attractive/more interesting than your friend, does she really need all the gory details? (Indeed, the whole sex and friendship thing is such a loaded subject that there's a whole chapter about it later.)

Some people use honesty as an excuse to whittle down your self-confidence with a series of nasty digs – all presented as helpful advice, of course. One way to test whether a friend is doing this is to think about the way you feel after seeing her. If you always feel worse than you did before you went out (and not because you decided that going for a fifth tequila would be a good idea), then maybe that person isn't quite the friend that you thought they were. If, on the other hand, you look back at

Friendship: The Basics

the criticisms your friend has given you and can see changes you've made for the better as a result, then they're probably being helpful.

Of course, it could be you that's guilty of using honesty as an excuse to attack a friend. If so, stop it right now. It's passive-aggressive and no way to behave. If you try to bring your friend down because you're jealous and think that they're better than you, work on your own confidence. Being successful in life, love or your career is about being yourself, not criticising or belittling other people who've achieved their success. And clearly, you must have attributes that your friend admires, because otherwise they wouldn't put up with such outrageous treatment from you.

Tawny's story: She made me feel cheap

I'd been working at a new company for a couple of months, and didn't really know anyone that well, so when Bella, one of the marketing managers, befriended me, I felt relieved. We took to going to lunch together most days and she encouraged me to see her as a mentor (even though she wasn't one of my bosses) as she'd been in the business for a lot longer than I had. It was useful for me to have someone I could question about things outside the office, and, at first, I was really grateful for her help.

Over coming months, I paid attention to what she said and it paid off – I got a promotion. But from then on, her behaviour seemed to change. Whereas before she'd been giving me

You Must Be My Best Friend ...

objective advice on things like the right way to write a report, now she was a lot more personal. She told me that I didn't dress in the right way to be taken seriously as a professional, but when I went out and bought a whole new wardrobe based on her advice, she didn't give me any positive feedback. Instead, she started making comments about how messy my desk was. My job was demanding so it was fair enough to say that there were times when my desk was piled up with papers, but I made sure that everything was filed at the end of each working day, so it really hurt that she was making comments like that – and now she was doing it in front of other people in the office, rather than over our lunches, so it was potentially damaging to my career.

I began to feel less and less motivated, thinking that nothing I could do was right. When I talked to Bella about it, she told me that I'd have to get used to dealing with stress if I was ever going to be a success.

Things came to a head when my manager called me into her office. I broke down and told her how I felt I wasn't right for the company: that I dressed badly and felt disorganised. She said that I was talking nonsense and that she was really happy with my progress – she was just worried about me because I'd lost so much confidence, and wanted to check that I was happy. We had a long conversation about work and I left feeling far more motivated.

Thinking about it afterwards, I realised that Bella had become intimidated by my rapid success and her comments said more about her than they did about me. The next time she asked me out to lunch, I said I was too busy. Over time, I made

Friendship: The Basics

a point of drifting apart from her and getting new friends who weren't trying to score points and boost their own egos by putting me down. It still scares me that I didn't realise how nasty she was until it was almost too late.

Trust me, I'm your friend

You'd think that expecting trust would be pretty much given as read. But what if you have two close friends and one confides that she's done something that could seriously hurt the other friend — say, going for her job, kissing her boyfriend or spreading a piece of gossip about her? What you do is partly down to loyalty — but sometimes it's not easy to pick where your loyalty should lie.

If a friend starts to tell you something and you don't think you'll be able to keep her confidence, tell her. That way, she knows that she needs to turn to someone else to discuss the issue, and you won't get caught between two friends. Plus, stopping her at the earliest possible stage means that you have less gossip that you need to keep to yourself.

Mia's story: I was caught in the middle

A couple of years ago, I became friends with Tim. I met him at the gym, and, although I initially fancied him, we became friends instead because he was married. I invited him and his wife over

You Must Be My Best Friend ...

to dinner because I enjoyed his company but didn't want her to think that I was after her man. Soon, I was chatting to her just as much as I chatted to him. He was great to talk to about sport – not to mention getting introductions to all his foxy friends at the gym. She was much quieter but really interesting – we'd have deep conversations about psychology. I saw Tim a bit more often, as Pam, his wife, didn't go to the gym, but I considered them both to be equally good friends of mine.

Then Tim dropped a bombshell on me. One day, when we were in the juice bar after training, he said that he was having an affair. He swore me to secrecy but said that he was seriously considering leaving Pam and wanted my advice. I didn't know what to say – they seemed perfect together to me – but at the same time didn't want to be a bad friend to Tim. In the end, I just listened to him talk about the other woman, and said that only he could decide what to do.

A few weeks later, Pam and I were having coffee together and she burst into tears. She told me that she thought Tim was having an affair, and asked whether I knew anything about it. I didn't think that I should be the one to tell her but, at the same time, felt really guilty keeping it secret. I think she even suspected that it might have been me, because I was so evasive whenever she got onto the subject.

This carried on for a few weeks – every time I saw Tim, he wanted a 'safe ear' to talk to, and every time I saw Pam, she wanted proof that Tim was cheating on her. In the end, I cancelled my gym membership and avoided both of their calls. I missed

Friendship: The Basics

both of them but there was no way that I wanted to get involved in someone else's relationship, and keeping Tim's confidence was killing me.

Loyalty

A good friend is expected to be loyal. However, as the above example illustrates, sometimes there can be a conflict between loyalty and trust. And different people have different perceptions of what loyalty is. One person may see it as disloyal if you're friends with anyone that they don't like, while another could consider it a betrayal if they get sacked from the company that you work at, and you don't walk out in protest at the way they've been treated (even if, deep down, you think it was the right decision).

As a general guide, be as loyal to your friends as you'd expect them to be to you. If you'd be gutted at the idea of a friend dating one of your exes, make sure that you don't do it to them, because double standards just aren't fair. By behaving in the same way you'd like to be treated, at the very least, you'll never be able to be accused of being a hypocrite. And with any luck, you'll be a good friend.

Lydia's story: Wedding hell

I'd been best friends with Jemma for 15 years, when she started going out with Stuart. I thought he was fantastic for her from day one, and she was pleased that he and I got on really well. Over the seven years that they were together, he and I got close enough that, if Jemma was away and we were both at a loose end, we could happily enjoy an evening together. So when they split up, I was almost as upset as they were about it. Jemma had been, and always would be my best friend, but Stuart was important to me too.

Jemma said that it was fine with her if I wanted to carry on being his friend – she didn't think it was fair to make me choose – but I always felt a bit uncomfortable about telling her if he and I had gone out, particularly when his new girlfriend was out with us too. I felt like I was betraying her.

But it wasn't until I received a wedding invitation from Stuart and Anne – his new girlfriend – that I realised I had to make a choice. I knew that, no matter how much she said it was OK, Jemma would be heartbroken if I, her best mate, went to the love of her life's wedding, as she was still besotted with him. And so I made a choice. I said I couldn't go. This led to a huge row between Stuart and I, which culminated in me telling him that I thought it would be best if we didn't see each other again, for Jemma's sake.

He was annoyed that 'Jemma got all the friends' after the split but, deep down, I think he must have realised that I couldn't turn my back on someone who'd been in my life for so much longer than he had, and who I cared so deeply about. I still miss him but I don't regret my decision. At least now I can talk openly with Jemma about what I've done at the weekend, rather than pretending I haven't seen Stuart and Anne in case I hurt her.

Friendship: The Basics

You're such a good laugh

Having a sense of humour is all very well, but different people find different things funny — there's nothing that is universally amusing. Chances are, you'll have a similar sense of humour to your friends, but be wary around areas of contention: sex, politics and religion, for example. You may have a fantastic joke about the Pope, but your Catholic friend may see it as far from funny.

As a rule, if in any doubt, don't. Something that you see as slightly near the knuckle could be really hurtful to someone else. And it should go without saying that you should never make cruel jokes at a friend's expense — at least, not if you want to keep them.

Elizabeth's story: Our joke backfired

Everyone in our group of mates used to joke about Kelly and another friend, Miles. They were both attached but they flirted with each other loads, so the running gag in the group was that they had something going on. We all knew they'd never really cheat on their partners - it was just one of those silly things that we'd banter about. So when Valentine's Day rolled around, a couple of us thought it would be a giggle to send a fake Valentine card to Kelly, apparently signed by Miles.

We sent it to her work so that her partner wouldn't see it and think that it was serious, and deliberately picked the most hideous stuffed and padded card with a kitten on the front, so she'd know that it was a joke – Miles was Mr Sophistication and would never send anything that was so tasteless.

Valentine's Day rolled around and halfway through the day, I gave Kelly a call at work. 'So, get any cards?' I casually asked.

'Yes,' she said, and burst into tears. 'Miles sent me one.'

I was really worried at her reaction so decided that the best thing to do would be to come clean and admit that we'd sent it to her. She was mortified and thought that we were deliberately picking on her. What we had meant to be a casual and friendly joke resulted in making her feel incredibly upset. She didn't come out with us for a few months afterwards and even now we're friends again, after a lot of apologies and working at it, she's a lot more muted around Miles because she thought that we were really suggesting that they should get together – or that they had cheated on their partners with each other in the past.

Now, I wouldn't play a practical joke on a friend unless I was absolutely certain that they wouldn't take it in the wrong way. Our joke was meant affectionately, and the last thing we wanted to do was upset Kelly, but a silly prank wasn't worth the pain it caused.

Come here and have a hug

Compassion is surprisingly low down the list, when you consider the many shades of grey in the attributes above it. Being prepared to listen to your friend offload her woes, give her a

Friendship: The Basics

hug or a bar of chocolate when she's feeling insecure or lend her the money for a burger when she's starving after a night out and has run out of cash is basic friendship.

However, being someone's friend doesn't mean that they are your responsibility. Everyone should take responsibility for their own life and trying to micro-manage your friend's behaviour because they're flaky isn't helpful at all.

It can be easy to fall into the trap of constantly taking control — man-handling your friend into a cab after yet another drunken night out, or calling her repeatedly to remind her that she's got to be at the cinema at 7pm if she doesn't want to miss the film again — because it takes less time and hassle than relying on a ditzy friend. But, to sound all motherly, if you don't let someone make their own mistakes, how will they ever learn? Obviously, you should never leave a friend in a dangerous situation (unless you're both at risk and the only hope of fixing it is for you to separate) but you needn't feel that you have to run a friend's life for them. Instead, make them aware of their own behaviour and encourage them to sort it out for themselves.

A good friend will offer advice, when asked, but won't be offended or upset if that advice is ignored. Obviously, there are exceptions, such as if someone has a drink or drug problem or is stuck in an abusive relationship, but these complex issues are covered separately later in the book. The most important thing, regardless of the situation, is to offer as much support as you can without putting yourself under too much strain, physically, mentally or emotionally.

You Must Be My Best Friend ...

Angie's story: She tried to control me with 'compassion'

One of my best friends from high school was a very controlling person. After high school, I moved out on my own and, after being sheltered my whole life, I was ready to party. There was this guy that I was sleeping with, and we were both cool with a 'just sex' relationship. My friend, however, was not. She would constantly corner me at parties at his house and tell me how I should stop seeing him, and that if I wouldn't, she couldn't be my friend any more. I repeatedly told her that true friends do not put limitations on their friendship, so if she couldn't accept that I'd choose the people I slept with, then I didn't want to be her friend. She said that the decisions I made for my own life affected her life, and that I wasn't being considerate of her feelings.

She was so obsessed with it that she would drive by my house to see if my car was there. If it wasn't, she would drive over to his house to see if my car was there. If it was, she would continue to drive around until I left. Then, she would call me the next day and say something like, 'What were you doing at his house until 3am?' She was a borderline stalker, as far as I was concerned. And, no, she wasn't a lesbian - she was engaged!

We worked together at a restaurant, and she would always make comments to other people about how I was sleeping with him. When I confronted her about talking badly about me, she told me that she told other people about it because she was angry that I wasn't confiding in her any more.

Friendship: The Basics

I eventually stopped returning her phone calls, and stopped hanging out with her - she was crazy. We did later become friends again - at the request of our mutual friends - but I told her I could only be her friend from a distance. I couldn't share any intimate details of my life with her any more.

After that experience, I realised that what I see as true friendship is someone who will stand by you, even when they disagree with the choices you make. I think a friend should definitely express their opinions and give advice, when solicited, but ultimately, they should respect your decisions and be there for you.

Of course, it could be that you're the unreliable friend who makes constant demands for attention and/or expects someone else to run your life for you. Compassion is about caring but not about caring *for* someone. You're a grown-up and you can make decisions on your own, no matter how hard it may seem. By all means, ask your friends for support when things are going badly, and ask their advice if they know more about a situation you're involved with than you do. But if you find yourself calling your best friend to ask what to wear every morning, stop being so self-indulgent, and get a grip. Don't be too hard on yourself about it though. A lot of the time this kind of behaviour comes from insecurity, so realise that you are a good person and you are capable of making your own decisions. If you work on your confidence, you'll be surprised at how much

You Must Be My Best Friend ...

you can cope on your own — and how much more willing friends will be to offer you support when things really do go wrong.

Alice's story: He helped me get over my painful past

When I was a child, I had a really rough time of it, the worst of which was getting abused by my uncle. It took me a long time to face what had happened and, even when I eventually realised it was abuse, I still blamed myself. Matters weren't helped when I told my first boyfriend about it. He thought that he was the one who'd taken my virginity, and when I confessed that it had been my uncle, when I was a child, his response was to call me a slut. After that, I was reticent about telling anyone what had happened to me, and went back to believing everything that had happened was my own fault.

About three years later, I met Andrew. We soon became close friends and, after we'd known each other really well for a couple of years, I felt brave enough to tell him what had happened. We were in a bar together and drinks had been flowing. Something he'd said had made me think that I needed to share what had happened to me with him, but I was still shaking as I started to speak.

As I told my story, he sat there, gradually going paler. Before long, I stopped what I was saying and asked, 'Do you hate me?' He said 'No, I hate the evil bastard who did that to you, babes.'

Friendship: The Basics

He gave me a huge hug and let me keep talking until I'd said everything that I'd been wanting to for years. He was totally understanding, at no point shying away from the conversation, and made me feel accepted.

To this day, I think that he was the most important part of my recovery. His caring reaction showed me that I wasn't a bad person, and made our friendship even closer than it had been before. Without him, I don't think I'd have been able to move on from my traumatic past.

Fun

If you don't have fun with your friends, to be blunt, what are you doing with them? Enjoying each other's company is an integral part of friendship (like, duh!). That said, you might have different interests to your friends. If so, take time to introduce them to your hobbies — yoga, attending a reading group or whatever — and ask them if they'd like to share their hobbies with you. It's all about balance rather than foisting your desires on your friends, or meekly agreeing to do whatever they suggest. You never know, by sharing hobbies, you may find new and interesting ways to have fun with each other — there are only so many hours that can be spent shopping, after all. Then again, you may hate their hobbies, and vice versa. If that's the case, don't panic. It doesn't mean that your friendship is doomed in any way. Friends don't have to be identical to you, after all — just think how boring that would be. Enjoy

You Must Be My Best Friend ...

your hobbies with someone else that shares your passion — or be brave and go on your own, because you could find that you make new friends — and have fun with your old pals in the ways you always have.

Abby's story: We had more in common than I thought

I hadn't known Sharon for long - we'd met on the internet, and, from the point we first started talking to each other, the conversations ran long into the night. I wasn't sure if it was just an internet thing, so we arranged to meet up and we got on just as well in person. After only a month, we were talking every day so when another friend asked me to house-sit her seaside home and said I could bring someone with me if I wanted, Sharon instantly sprang to mind.

Our main topic of conversation was always men, so I wasn't sure if she'd enjoy being stuck in the depths of the seaside, out of season, with no clubs in the area. But she eagerly agreed, and I looked forward to a week of us finding all the local talent at night, and lazing on the beach by day.

When we got there, Sharon said that she wasn't really in the mood to pull, and then admitted, in an embarrassed way, that she'd brought her binoculars to go birdwatching. I was shocked but pleasantly surprised. I'd always been a nature-girl at heart but was sure that Sharon would be bored out of her mind by it, so had set aside all thoughts of walks by the sea.

Friendship: The Basics

We ended up having a lovely week wandering along the beach looking at rock pools and admiring the stunning views. By inviting Sharon away with me, I'd learned about a whole new side of her and, even though at home, we keep each other's secret and pretend to be girls about town, it's definitely made us closer.

Love

When you think of how much time people devote to looking for love in a relationship, it's surprising that it's not higher up the list as a friendship attribute. After all, at root, love is caring about someone. Then again, it can feel a bit more embarrassing asking a friend, 'Do you love me?' or saying, 'I love you.' Instead, show that you care by treating your friend with respect and compassion. It's way less likely to freak them out than proposing marriage.

Zara's story: We love each other

I've known Cassie for ever and couldn't even begin to think what life would be like without her – we went to the same school, the same university and both moved to the same city after graduation. I can't think of anything we haven't talked about – she certainly knows all my dirty little secrets, and I'm pretty sure that I know all of hers. But, without meaning to lessen how important she is to me, I never thought of our relationship as being a particularly special thing – she's just Cas, and she's part of my life.

Then, one night, when we were drunk, she said, 'You do know I love you, Zara?' I laughed it off as you do when a drunk pal goes, 'but I love you,' and she looked at me, soberly, and said, 'No, I really do. You're really important to me. Don't worry, I'm not a lezzer, but I love you.' I told her that I loved her too because I realised, at that moment, that I did – and much more than some of the bloke losers I've thought I've loved.

The next morning, neither of us mentioned it, but there have been other times – usually after too much to drink – when we've repeated ourselves. We don't tell each other all that often but we don't really need to. We both know how much we care about each other now, and it makes me smile just thinking about it.

Understanding

It's not always easy to understand a friend's behaviour: why she carries on dating a loser, insists that puce is the ideal colour for her bridesmaids' dresses (which you'll have to wear) or stays in a job that she hates but whines about every day. Sometimes it's best to ask her to explain her reasoning to help you understand, particularly if she's doing something that is out of character. At other times, your best option is to keep your mouth shut (particularly where her taste in partners is

Friendship: The Basics

involved). You can show understanding – smiling and nodding – without *actually* understanding a friend's motivations. And if her choices aren't hurting anyone, including herself, then a little white lie of faked understanding can go a long way.

Simone's story: He was clueless about his nightmare girlfriend

Maxwell was a real sweetheart. We met through my boyfriend, and got on almost as well with each other as I did with my other half – albeit without any sexual attraction. Maxwell loved the same comedians as I did, and we often spent evenings making each other laugh or talking long into the night. My boyfriend had mentioned that Maxwell's girlfriend, Selene, was a bit of a nightmare but I couldn't see that anyone Maxwell hung round with could be that bad because he was just so nice.

I couldn't have been more wrong. When I met Selene, she snootily looked me up and down, then, blanking me, turned to Maxwell and sent him to buy her a drink. When he offered me one too, she barked, 'You can't afford it,' at him. He looked mortified.

Because Maxwell was so keen on her, I tried to make an effort – double-dating with him would have been great were it not for Selene. But I soon realised that she was a total man's woman. Whenever my boyfriend was around, she'd smile sweetly and talk to him, so he thought I was overreacting, but when she and I were alone, she was cold. And even worse, she faked being stupid in front of the guys: something that really winds me up.

No matter how hard I looked for the good in her, I couldn't understand what Maxwell saw in her, but I knew he'd be upset if I told him I hated her so I kept my mouth shut whenever her name cropped up.

Eventually, she dumped Maxwell - it turned out she'd been cheating on him. Even though he was upset, I was glad that such a nasty woman was out of my friend's life, and it made it a lot easier for us to have an honest friendship.

I'm listening

One cliché that's well worth remembering is that we have two ears and one mouth, and should use them accordingly. Listening to a friend as much as you talk is essential. And make sure it's 'active listening' – saying 'So he did that – and then what?' or giving lots of conversational prompts like 'go on' – not just smiling and nodding until the point at which you can say your piece. Most people are guilty of only half listening at some stage, particularly if they're distracted by something else – recovering after a hard day's work or even just having the TV on in the background.

Similarly, if a friend is offloading, try not to turn it into something that's all about you. The following conversation is best avoided:

Friendship: The Basics

Friend: I'm really worried about Jack — I think he's seeing someone else.
You: That sounds just like Stuart. Did I tell you about the time that I thought he was seeing the barmaid at our local, and it turns out he was?

Being self-centred is human nature — or at least everyone is selfish to some extent — but if you're never able to sympathise with your friend without using an example from your own life to empathise with her, you're heading for a one-way friendship, and accusations of believing the world revolves around you. And that isn't the case now, is it?

Bet's story: She came first

When Catriona split up with her boyfriend, John, I happened to be there. I was the only girl in the group of us out that night, so it seemed to fall to me to look after her, even though there were other people in the group that she knew better than me. She and I were friends, just not that close, and I didn't mind. After all, we've all been there, and I knew that the blokes were rubbish at handling a woman in tears.

Catriona ended up coming back to mine that night, and in the morning I said that if she ever needed to call, she could - and call she did. Sometimes, she'd phone me four or five times in a day to go over the same stuff again and again. I felt responsible - I'd said I'd be there for her and I couldn't exactly hang up on her. Even when she called me at 7am on a Saturday, I picked up.

You Must Be My Best Friend ...

Luckily, after a month, she met someone else and started to put herself back together. We still talked lots - the experience had brought us closer and she said she was really grateful for everything I'd done. Whenever the group of us went out, she and I would end up chatting and it was nice having a girlie ally in the group - particularly when the boys decided drinking games were a good idea and we weren't in the mood, because we could back each other up.

About six months later, I split up with my boyfriend, Alexander. We'd been together for four years so I was devastated. Catriona was the first person I called but she said she had to go after five minutes. The next night, the group of us had arranged to meet up and I decided to brave it, even though all I wanted to do was curl up in bed. I thought that Catriona would help me through it but she was really weird with me all night. Every time I tried to bring up Alexander, she'd offer to get me a drink or cigarettes, and she'd leave the table. When I asked if I could stay at hers, she said her boyfriend was staying over - she wasn't even that apologetic.

After a couple more weeks of this, I realised that she only wanted a friend when she needed help - she just couldn't listen to other people's problems. She was sweet in some ways - buying me drinks and trying to get me out of the house - but any time I got emotional, she was embarrassed. Part of me hated her because it was so different from the way I'd treated her but, in hindsight, I've realised she's just not very

Friendship: The Basics

good at talking about anyone else's problems. She's much more someone I see as a lightweight mate than proper friend now.

Kindness

Being kind to your friends should be taken as read. If you're mean to them, you're a crap friend. But, as with compassion, make sure you're not so kind that you're running your friend's life for her, or getting taken for granted. Being kind and being controlling or put upon are entirely different things.

Ellie's story: My flatmate made my life hell

When I first moved in with Debra, I thought she was brilliant fun. She was always going to glamorous parties and getting invitations for me. She introduced me to her friends, gave me full access to her designer wardrobe, and generally made me feel welcome. I thought I'd got a new best friend, particularly because I'd just moved to a new town so didn't really know that many people there.

To say thanks, I got into the habit of cooking for us. I enjoy cooking so it wasn't that big a deal for me to make enough for two. One night, about a month after I'd started doing this, I got a call from her when I was working late. 'What time are you coming home?' she asked. 'I'm hungry.' Suddenly, my 'thanks for the parties' gesture had turned into something that she

You Must Be My Best Friend ...

expected. I told her I'd be working until a lot later, but rather than apologising for interrupting, she asked me to let her know if it was likely to happen again so that she could make her own arrangements. She sounded annoyed with me for messing up her day by daring to work late. Part of me was irritated but I put it down to stress.

A couple of weeks later, I heard a panicked banging on my door at four in the morning. I scrambled out of bed to see Debra, in tears. 'What's wrong?' I asked, thinking that she'd been attacked or we'd got a burglar. 'I've got three wasps in my room and I don't like them. Can you get rid of them?' she begged. I was furious. It wasn't like she was allergic to them. She just didn't want to deal with it and thought that, as her friend, it was my job. But somehow, I still found myself trying to catch them and get them out of her window anyway.

After that, I decided it was time to move out. I felt more like her mother than her friend, and didn't want to have to look after another person when I had enough to cope with settling into a new town myself.

* * *

With a list of friedship attributes that long, it's a wonder that any of us have friends at all. But you shouldn't expect to get everything you need from one friend; you should be able to be self-sufficient, but get different forms of satisfaction

Friendship: The Basics

from different people. You may have one pal you can trust with your darkest secret, but know she's a bit of a tightwad. Another friend could have you doubled up in hysterics every time you see her but couldn't possibly deal with you breaking down in tears. That doesn't mean that either of those people is lacking as a friend – it's just that, being human, they're not perfect.

Catherine's story: It depends on the friend

I find I adapt myself to other people's idea of friendship. For example, being friends with Sally means when she introduces me to the latest love of her life and I find he looks like a rodent with questionable hygiene, an IQ of 49 and is quite possibly an alcoholic, I can say, 'What are you seeing in him? He just told me he's half American, half Canadian and half Russian, when he's quite clearly born and bred in the East End of London and smells of pickles,' and she'll laugh and tell me he's great in bed/rich/has handy apartment close to her fave nightclub.

If my friend Gill introduced the same bloke to me and I said this she would never speak to me again. Instead, I'd say, 'Yes ... he seems ... friendly,' or something equally vague and only after they had split up would it be acceptable for me to say, 'Oh, I never liked him ...'

Personally I prefer the honest approach. I'd much rather be told by someone that my arse looks massive in the trousers I am trying on than to be told I look lovely and then have an epiphany

You Must Be My Best Friend ...

after weeks of wearing them and realise I've been walking round with my arse looking massive, which could have been prevented if I had been forewarned.

As long as you treat each other with respect and don't feel bad after seeing each other, then you've got the basis of a healthy friendship. So just relax and go with the flow. And above all, bear in mind that friendship is a two-way street. If you treat your friends in the way that you'd like them to treat you, chances are you won't go too far wrong.

Elizabeth's story: Don't expect everything from one person

You can't get everything from one person, so different friends are important to satisfy different parts of your personality. Friendship is having someone to talk to who won't judge you and someone to laugh with - someone to share life with. I also believe guys and girls can be friends. My friends include current work mates, friends I have met through mutual acquaintances and family the same age as me.

I expect a friend to be someone you can talk to honestly and not have to compete with (especially when you are woman). They should be someone who will support you, send you silly emails, who will come with you to events you enjoy, make you laugh and be mature enough to share their opinions, even if they

Friendship: The Basics

don't agree with yours. Someone who gives you your space and doesn't get upset that you haven't called them in a fortnight.

When I was younger I thought friendships would last for ever and that every friend I had would have to be close to me for me to count them as a friend. As I've got older I've realised that a lot of people come in and out of your life and that you are friends with some people on a lighter scale than others. Some people call their milkman their friend. It's made me realise that I should cherish what I have when I have it, no matter how big or small it is, not expect friendships to last a lifetime and appreciate the little ones as well as the big ones.

GOLDEN RULES FOR FRIENDSHIP

1. Be honest – but not too honest. If your best pal says, 'Does my bum look big in this?' the answer is never 'yes', but it is sometimes, 'God, they're really badly cut – those ones you tried on earlier were much sexier.'
2. Make an effort: Ensure that you invite friends out as much as they invite you out. No one likes doing all the running.
3. Be an individual: Don't just go along with what your friends suggest. Friendship isn't passive, and anyone who likes you because they get their own way the whole time isn't a real friend.
4. Don't try to take over your friend's life – let her make her own mistakes.

You Must Be My Best Friend ...

5. Never expect anything of a friend that you wouldn't be prepared to do for her.
6. Trust your friends and don't do anything to betray their trust. Sure, sometimes you'll get let down but better that than never entering fully into friendship.
7. Listen as much as you talk. Friendship is a two-way exchange.
8. If a friend does something that upsets you, tell her. Inwardly seething won't do your relationship any good at all.
9. If you make a mistake, apologise. Trying to hide it will just make things worse. Except when it comes to drunkenly snogging their bloke at a party ...
10. ... so never touch a mate's man. If you do, you can expect to lose a friend for good.

Chapter Two

The Life Cycle of Friendships

You might think that, once you'd got the basics covered, friendship would be easy, but you'd be making a mistake if you did. Knowing what kind of friends you have, and making sure that you treat them properly, is just one part of the story. Sadly, because friendships are about people, you have to deal with the fact that they can change. OK, some friends really will be there throughout your life, but bearing in mind the '6 friends out of 396 pals in a lifetime' figure, it's pretty obvious that you'll move on from the majority of people that you connect with.

Before you start making a mental list of the people you're going to strike off your 'friends for life' list, calm down. Most friendships don't end because of a huge row or otherwise dramatic event. They just evolve. The girl in accounts who you spend hours gossiping to right now could well drift out of your life if you move to another company. Or you might have a baby and suddenly become fixated with all things child-related, while

You Must Be My Best Friend ...

your best friend stays child-free and is bored out of her mind discussing nappy rash and the best baby buggy. And as you change, your friendships will change too.

Moving to a different part of the world or simply outgrowing someone can all mean that the person you love to bits as a friend right now might not be in your life in a year's time. Relax. This is normal. And if you really do want to keep someone in your life long-term, you can make it more likely to happen by working at the relationship (unless, of course, your friend is the one who decides they don't want to hang out with you any more, in which case there's only a certain amount of work that is worth putting in).

Lizzy's story: She turned into a liability

When I was 17, well brought up and fresh out of a loving home, I'd rebelled and moved into my own flat with my boyfriend. I met a girl, Julie, in an adjacent flat who was unemployed, smoked and swore. I thought it was really cool and she was great fun as well as being a nice person. I'd sneak over to her house for cigarettes without my boyfriend knowing. We were from very different social strata and I enjoyed hanging out on the 'wrong' side. We didn't have much in common but talked about what we did.

After a year or two I broke up with the boy and moved to another place but I kept in contact with my friend. I matured and

The Life Cycle of Friendships

realised I didn't want to be unemployed, got myself some training and a good job. About five years later I was still visiting Julie but I started to feel like a social worker. She had had a lovely child but we had absolutely nothing in common to talk about any more. She never had transport so I was always visiting her, and I couldn't tell her anything about work because she thought I was stuck up. All she talked about was unemployment benefits and child rearing.

I felt terrible in making the decision to not see her any more but knew I had to do it. I wasn't getting anything out of the relationship. I started to drop off contact. She would ring and ask me if anything was wrong and I would deny it. I couldn't tell her I didn't want to be her friend any more. But then I realised that I owed it to her so, instead of ignoring her in the hope she would go away, I decided to write her a two-page letter. I wrote to her saying how I had really enjoyed her company over the years and wished her well but that we didn't have any connection any more. I felt bad about leaving her but felt better that I gave her a reason and she knew about it, instead of always wondering why I didn't visit her any more.

I moved out of the area and about four years later moved back again. I saw her in the shopping centre with her little boy and pretended I didn't see her. I don't know if she saw me but she looked happy.

I have had friends dump me by not returning calls and avoiding me, and it hurts. When I did talk to them they were as nice as pie to my face (guilt?) so you just don't know what's going

You Must Be My Best Friend ...

on. I think when you have a good relationship with someone and you want to call it off, you owe it to them to explain why. If you can't do it face to face, then write a letter. You'll finish everything with both you feeling relieved and not so hurt by the separation.

Some people think that, in order to be friends, you need to see each other every day, or at least every week. As such, if they don't see a friend for a few months for some reason, they'll assume that the friendship is over. This is counter-productive. With long working hours and more stuff than ever before to fit into your life (Brazilian waxes, pilates, organic food shopping – who invented all this time-consuming so-called 'essential' stuff?), sometimes friendships can go on the back burner. There's no reason why, after a long gap, you should feel too guilty about neglecting your friend to pick up the phone and call her. After all, she hasn't called you either – probably because she was too busy maintaining her hectic diary of Brazilian waxes and pilates as well. Even if you do have a huge backlog of calls from her that you haven't responded to, it's nothing that you can't deal with if the friendship is strong enough. Just grovel and take her out to lunch, with you settling the bill by way of apology. And don't do it again.

Similarly, if you've totally lost contact with an old friend who you miss, don't be scared to try to get back in touch; there's a good chance that they miss you too. According to

The Life Cycle of Friendships

research by BT, 6 million people every year attend school reunions in the UK alone, and 39 per cent of us would like to re-establish a friendship with a former schoolmate. Almost half the people in that survey said they dream about old friends, with a quarter doing so on a regular basis. So just pick up the phone or follow the lead of the majority (72 per cent) and do an internet search. Technology has made it much easier to find people. And who knows, you may find that your friendship is just as strong as adults as it was when you were kids. Even if it isn't, at least you won't be left wondering 'what if?' and hating yourself for neglecting someone you cared about.

No matter how often you see someone and how much your life changes, it is possible to maintain friendships if you have a strong enough emotional bond to make it worthwhile. Most of the common problems a friendship encounters can be dealt with easily, as long as you're prepared to make an effort.

COPING WITH A CHANGE OF LIFESTYLE

The most common reason that friends drift apart is a change of lifestyle. People tend to hang around with others who are similar. So, in student days, you may find it easy to make friends; most teenagers want the same thing – parties, drinks, sex and (probably) a qualification at the end of their studies. But once you hit the 'real world' other things come into play. You're not necessarily going to live just round the corner from

You Must Be My Best Friend ...

your friends any more, so spending time with each other takes more effort. And, chances are, your social life will be a bit more varied than hanging out in the student union bar or local teen nightclub, so discovering that you and your friends have different tastes in the way you want to spend your free time will have an impact too.

There are also huge changes in lifestyle between your teens and early twenties. Friends are all-important as a teenager, but as you get older, more life pressures come into play. Work and relationships vie for your time, and you may start to get into the whole family thing.

As a general rule, single women tend to mix with other singles, couples meet up with other couples and parents mix with other parents. It's a practical choice – you tend to have more in common with people who are in a similar life state. And, in some ways, you're more likely to be able to help someone with a problem if you've been through it yourself.

However, that's only really useful information when it comes to making new friends. Problems start to creep in when a good friend who has been in the same situation as you suddenly changes her lifestyle. She might develop a love of clubbing in a desperate attempt to cling on to her youth, where previously she's been a strictly dinner-parties-and-cosy-nights-in kind of girl. It might be that she gets pregnant or finds true love. She might come out, or decide that she wants to be an eco-warrior and bin the shopping trips you go on because they support the evils of capitalism. She might even win the lottery and start to

The Life Cycle of Friendships

hang out with the 'beautiful people' (before whe realises that money doesn't make a personality). Or any of these things could happen to *you* and your friends could be left wondering what happened to the 'you' they knew and loved.

Emma's story: They've turned dull

One of the guys in my group of friends and his fiancée are expecting a baby, and already they're boring! They won't plan anything for the summer or anything 'because of the baby' ... Geesh, I don't even want to think of what it'll be like once the kid's out.

While humans are adaptable, most of us aren't all that keen on change and you need to be prepared to let your friendships evolve if you're going to maintain them. Rather than getting bitter about the way that your friend has changed, try to empathise. Maybe she felt stuck in a rut as the 'old her' and felt like she needed to grow up — or that she needed to throw caution to the wind and act like a big kid. It could be that you've got so used to seeing your friend in a particular way that you haven't noticed her gradually evolving. Or perhaps it's just a phase she's going through. If you have enough in common at a deeper level than just enjoying each other's company at parties or out shopping then a change of lifestyle shouldn't affect the friendship.

You Must Be My Best Friend ...

Sometimes, people panic about a friend changing because they feel that it adversely reflects on them. If your best pal gets a mortgage and moves her boyfriend in, you might feel subconsciously that you're lagging behind her in the 'game of life' and, as such, invert those feelings so that it becomes about her rather than you. If you find yourself sniping about her spending another weekend at the DIY store, or complaining that she isn't the same person she used to be – hang back. Look at her behaviour from an objective point of view. Is it that you got used to her being around for you whenever you called, and now you're annoyed that something else takes precedence over you? If so, you need to accept that things change, and plan things with her in advance. Like it or not, the world doesn't revolve around you.

However, if you keep arranging to go out together and your friend then cancels at the last minute because she's got her boyfriend's parents coming round, you need to have a chat with her about fair behaviour. If you've set aside time for her by mutual agreement, she's taking advantage of you by cancelling at the last minute. Don't be too rough on her though; adapting behaviour is just as hard for the person who's going through it – if not harder – as it is for those around them.

The most important thing to remember is that people don't stay the same for ever. Everything that happens in life has an impact on a person, and if we didn't change, it would be unhealthy. However, by talking to your friend, and paying attention to what she says – and vice versa – you should be able

The Life Cycle of Friendships

to spot the changes and either adapt accordingly, or move on to another friend who shares your lifestyle. Do bear in mind that hanging around with a group of clones will get boring eventually though; it makes much more sense to have a varied mixture of friends as, that way, you'll have a far broader social sphere and will still have friends who enjoy hanging out with you no matter how much *you* change.

Alix's story: Work changed everything

I used to work in the comedy industry, arranging gigs for aspiring stand-ups. I met Lily at one of the events – she was an agent and represented new talent. It turned out that we had lots of mutual acquaintances and we struck up a friendship. Comedy is quite male-dominated so it was nice to have another woman in the industry to talk to. We'd see each other out and about at gigs a few times a week and, as she lived near me, we ended up going out socially most weekends too. I definitely counted her as one of my best friends.

After a few years, I got bored of the amount of sexism in the industry and decided to change careers. My new job was pretty intense – I had to prove myself as I was effectively starting over, aged 35. This meant that I didn't get to see Lily anything like as much as I had before. When we eventually found a weekend where we were both free, I was really looking forward to seeing her. But I was disappointed to discover, after several hours of trying to make conversation, that all we had ever talked about before was work. It hadn't felt like that at the time, but it wasn't until we fell back on the old topic of what was going on in comedy, with her filling me in on all the industry gossip, that we had a conversation that flowed rather than felt like small talk. I put it down to us having a gap between seeing each other, and thought that things would get back to the way they were before the next time we saw each other. But when we met up again, it was just as bad. Conversation was stilted and we didn't really know what to say to each other.

The last thing I wanted to do was talk about the career I'd got out of – by the time I ended my job, I'd hated it, and half the people in the business. But she wasn't all that interested in my new career either – it was alien to her.

We still see each other about once a year, but sadly, I think that's about all the friendship can cope with. We just don't know each other well enough for it to get any deeper. I could only see the friendship getting back to what it once was if I went back into comedy, and there's no way that I'm ever going to do that.

COPING WITH A CHANGE OF STATUS

Sometimes, a change of lifestyle brings with it a change of status. When you're in your teens or early twenties, it's likely that you'll be in a similar financial position to your friends. As such, your evenings out will be designed around your

The Life Cycle of Friendships

budget. But when people get older, there can be more of a diversity of income: one person could follow their vocation and be earning a pittance, while another is earning a fortune doing a job they hate. A lucky few will earn a decent salary doing a job that they love — George Clooney's make-up artist for nude scenes, or international rock-star, say — but they're few and far between.

With differing pay packets comes a whole host of problems (dealt with in chapter three). But money isn't the only way that status changes can affect a friendship. If your best friend gets a high-powered job, she may well end up working all hours. All of a sudden, she doesn't want to go out during the week, and calling her late at night when you're having a crisis becomes an issue. This can lead to resentment and feelings that your friend is putting her job first. You may feel that she's changed beyond all recognition and is now a career woman rather than the party animal you knew and loved.

One coping mechanism is to mentally reverse the situation. Imagine that you're in the position your friend is in, and think about the way you'd like people to respond to that change. For example, if her demanding job means that late nights in bars are out during the week, move them to a Saturday (having given her Friday to relax after her hard time at work) and you'll probably find that your wild friend is still there underneath her business suit.

Explain the way that you feel to her as well; she probably misses you just as much as you miss her, and you could find a

You Must Be My Best Friend ...

solution like spending lunch hours chatting to each other on the phone or over instant messenger will help you both maintain the friendship.

Another good trick is to call up your friend at short notice. It doesn't always work but, a lot of the time, people who are busy with work don't have the time to plan anything socially, and then find themselves sitting in on a Saturday night watching TV. So if you call her on a Saturday afternoon, you've got a higher chance of getting to see her than if you ask her earlier in the week. At the opposite side of the spectrum, giving a lot of notice also works – asking her to book a date in her diary for you a month in advance – as that means that she can plan her workload accordingly: and it's a bigger deal for her to try to cancel if you've booked her up that far ahead. OK, messing around with people's guilt complexes is a bit mean, but needs must if you want to stay in contact with a busy mate.

If you're the one with a high-powered job, make sure that you prioritise staying in contact with your friends. If you don't have enough time to see all of your friends in person, catch up with them over the phone or email instead. It's not quite the same as a gossipy evening together but at least it shows that you're prepared to put some effort in, and don't see your job as being more important than they are.

If your friend lives or works near you do, arrange to have lunch together near the office, or drinks after work. Snatch every spare moment that you can. Even half an hour a week is better than no contact at all.

The Life Cycle of Friendships

Another good way to stay in touch with friends when you have a limited amount of time is to arrange big gatherings — parties or afternoons in the pub — where you can catch up with a group of friends in one go. It may not be as strong a way of maintaining the bond as one-to-one conversations with them all, but at least it means that you get to spend some time with your friends and find out what's going on in their lives. Otherwise, you could end up falling off your friends' radars — and then what are you going to do if life starts going pear-shaped or you lose your job?

No matter how busy or tired you are, it's important to keep in contact with people you care about. You can guarantee that, when you're on your deathbed, you won't be thinking, 'I wish I'd spent more time in the office.'

Kai's story: I'm a Sunday Girl

Ever since I was a teenager I've been passionate about work. No matter what job I've been in, I've ended up working ridiculously long hours because it's important to me to deliver the best work that I can. However, I didn't realise how much it had taken over my life until I went freelance. All of a sudden, I found myself working almost 24/7 - I was even working at 11pm most Saturday nights, just to cover everything I needed to do. I was scared of turning down commissions unless the next one never came along. Friends complained that they never got to see me,

You Must Be My Best Friend ...

and I lost count of the amount of times I had to reply to a friend's email saying, 'Sorry, things are really manic but be great to catch up soon,' – and then 'soon' never happening.

When I realised that I hadn't even allowed myself time to arrange my own birthday party, I decided that this had to stop. I got a book on time management and decided that weekends were my own: for seeing friends, tidying the flat and generally catching up on life.

It hasn't always worked perfectly – there are still times when a deadline takes precedence because it has to if I'm not going to lose a commission – but I now make a point of, at the very least, catching up with my friends over the phone on a Sunday. It shows them that I'm still thinking of them, even if I can't be with them, and also helps me feel like I still have some semblance of life underneath all the work.

I'm beginning to make a point of turning down projects now, because I want to make sure that I have enough time to spend with my friends. They're just as important as achieving career goals, if not more so. I'm just glad that I realised work was taking over my life when I did – otherwise, I don't think I'd have had any friends left to go out with at the end of the day.

Another change of status that can affect your friendship is splitting up with a partner. Meeting each other's friends is all part of a relationship, and it's pretty common for couples to end up having mutual pals. But if your long-term relationship ends, deciding who gets to 'keep the friends' is tough. It could well be that someone your ex-partner has known for ten years actually gets on better with you, but your ex will feel seriously betrayed if that friend 'takes sides' with you over the breakup.

Sadly, you need to accept that one of the downsides of a long-term relationship ending is that you may lose some friends. This can be particularly hurtful because you're already going through a time of stress, but don't see it as a judgement against you. It's just that some people find it hard to split their loyalty between two people, or hate the idea of being caught in the middle of a rowing couple so take the easy option instead.

Don't give up all hope though: it could be that the friendship can be rebuilt once the dust has settled. Give it time and have patience. A good time to try to re-establish friendships you've lost with mutual friends is once your ex has got a new partner and have been with them for a couple of months. Just make sure that you don't use the friendship as an excuse to get all the gossip on exactly how fat and unpleasant your ex's new partner is.

Cecillia's story: Blood is thicker than water

I'm 32 years old and have been divorced since 2003 after a seven-year marriage. I became really close to my husband's sister during the separation before the divorce. She and I were

You Must Be My Best Friend ...

always good friends but became much closer when her brother cheated on me. She developed into a best friend and stood by me through all the heartache, pain, grieving and dynamics of the situation. She truly helped me deal with it and was by my side whenever I felt that I couldn't take it any more.

We went out, had fun, spent a lot of time just enjoying and exploring our friendship. We shared our deepest thoughts and emotions, laughing, crying and doing the stereotypical 'best friend' activities. Basically, she sided with me against her brother and the tramp he was seeing. I felt that, if nothing else, my marriage was good for bringing her into my life and showing me a truly wonderful friendship.

Unfortunately, I failed to see what two of my oldest friends (whom I had known since the age of six) pointed out from the beginning: Blood is thicker than water.

So, to make a long story short, my sister-in-law began getting to know my husband's girlfriend behind my back. Eventually, she started cutting time she spent with me shorter and even started avoiding me by not replying to emails or phone calls. It felt as if I was being cheated on all over again. The heartache and painful emotions all came flooding back and seemed worse simply because it was now the dual agony of losing both my husband and my best friend to the same road-whore.

· I still have the two loyal friends in my life and they have helped me deal with this as best they can. The problem is that we live in different cities – but the one thing I can count on is

The Life Cycle of Friendships

that their friendship has stood the test of time. We have known each other since we started school: 26 years and counting. We have seen each other grow up, each into a different type of woman: one is a lawyer – single, dynamic, independent and a devout Christian; the other a secretary – married (and changed her religion when she got married) with two sons aged four and one, juggling a career with a demanding home life; and finally me in the IT industry – divorced, no kids, new boyfriend, unsure of where my life is going.

Our friendship is wonderful as we add value to each other's lives wherever the differences lie. We have shared experiences from our first training bra, first period, first sexual encounter, first alcoholic beverage and lots more. We have cried together many times and we have gotten in and out of trouble together countless times. We have been very angry at each other and have had uncomfortable moments but our friendship has overcome it all. We went through phases of putting men ahead of each other and bowing out in the hope that the man will bring happiness to a friend ... yet knowing that it was only a phase. We have been 'cruel to be kind' when drastic measures were called for. With time we have realised that our friendship does not rely on constant phone calls or emails. It is simply knowing that that friend will always be there. Whether we're in touch once a day, week, month or year, it's always as if there was no gap. We can always pick up where we left off as if no time has passed. So sod my ex sister-in-law, her brother and the horse he is now riding!

You Must Be My Best Friend ...

COPING WITH A CHANGE OF ADDRESS

Distance is another major factor in friendship. If you're used to seeing a friend all the time, even a small move to the next town can make a difference. Suddenly, you can't call her at 8pm to arrange to meet her in half an hour, and you need to start planning when you see each other in advance, which can be a nightmare if you've had a spontaneous friendship before.

Both of you need to work at the friendship in this scenario. Take it in turns to go to each other's houses, and consider getting a spare bed if you don't already have one, so that it's easy for your friend to stay over. And look on the bright side: with both of you living in different places, you've got two lots of local talent to eye up, two sets of shops nearby to max your credit card in – and if you totally embarrass yourself in your local, you can always go to her local instead.

If one of you decides to go travelling, it can be even tougher. Suddenly, the person who's been around for you isn't even in the same hemisphere. Contact can be tricky, with postcards, short phone calls and long emails as the only real options. And, chances are, if someone's travelling for more than a month or so, you'll both find yourself forming other friendships to fill the gap. This can cause problems when you get back together again (see chapter four on 'third-wheel syndrome'). Even at the time, it can be tough hearing about the fantastic night out that your best mate's had with someone who isn't you. Jealousy

The Life Cycle of Friendships

exists just as much in friendships as relationships – people just tend to mask their feelings more because it feels petty.

If you really miss your friend while she's away, you may want to consider taking some time off work and going to visit her. Even if you only spend a week together while she's away for a year, she'll be touched that you're prepared to make that much effort to spend time with her. Don't just surprise her though. Some people go travelling to escape from home and, much as she loves you, she may not want a reminder. It could also trigger her homesickness. But if she's game, then you get to see your best friend and have a holiday all at once, so it's got double the benefit (though make sure you read the section on holidaying with friends so it doesn't cause more problems than it solves).

Sari's story: People move on

I've gone travelling abroad for long periods of time a couple of times now, and it's actually quite sad to realise how all my friends had 'moved on' with their lives while I've been away. A couple of other people in similar circumstances I've talked to have reported the same thing. Of course one shouldn't expect everything to be as it was when left behind some months ago, but somehow it still comes as a shock to come back and realise that your friends have moved on and have new friends and hobbies and interests now. They might not even be that keen to

You Must Be My Best Friend ...

see you any more (or is it just me?), or, what's even worse, when you do see them again, you can't quite think of anything to talk about any more – even if you have been in touch with them a bit by snail mail or e-mails. This has happened with some very good friends of mine, and I'm now afraid to actually meet them again, in case I can't think of anything to talk about.

And then there's the biggie: moving to another country for good. With the internet making the world ever-smaller, it's not uncommon for people to get job offers abroad, or simply decide to up sticks and move away. Some people move countries to be with a new partner, and others decide that they can't cope with where they're living for one more second so decide to move on. This can be tough for the people left behind, as they can feel rejected. It also changes the nature of friendships, because it's hard to get a hug from someone a thousand miles away. But, as with all other changes, it isn't impossible to keep a strong friendship if you're prepared to put in some effort.

Tori's story: Thousands of miles made no difference

I'd been friends with Alex for years. We'd always got on well, but he changed from being a mate to a best friend when he helped me through my messy breakup with his best male friend.

The Life Cycle of Friendships

At one point, he not only talked me to sleep but also took phone calls from me at 6am when I woke up and felt awful. I'm pretty sure that I wouldn't have got through the breakup without him; at the time, I was going through bad depression and he pulled me out the other side. He was a true friend and I really appreciated what he'd done.

We only saw each other about once a month but chatted over instant messenger most days and had a weekly phone catch-up where we got to find out all the gossip. Whenever we went out, we had a great time but we were both busy with work and lived at opposite ends of a big city so it wasn't always practical to meet up face-to-face. Nonetheless, when he told me that he was moving to another country for work, I was gutted. He was someone I liked having around, and even if we didn't see each other that much, it was nice knowing that we could.

I went to his leaving party and had to hold back the tears at the thought of him going. But it turns out, there was no need to be worried. As soon as he got his new flat, he sent me his phone number, and after a bit of investigation, I realised that it wasn't all that much more expensive to call him on a landline overseas than it was calling him on his mobile phone in the same country. We still have long phone conversations and can chat over instant messenger whenever we want. Moving to a different country might have been a big deal a few years ago but now technology makes it so much easier to stay in contact that I sometimes forget he's not around the corner any more. Even better, there are enough cheap flights around that it only takes a bit of saving to be able to afford to see him. And I get a holiday overseas into the bargain.

It would be lovely if he still lived in this country but, to be honest, his move hasn't had that much of an impact on our friendship. I guess that we're close enough that it doesn't matter where in the world we both are.

Sorry mate, you're dumped

So, you can see that it's possible to keep a friendship going under all manner of different situations. But sometimes, you might not want to. Like it or not, people outgrow each other. People change at different paces and sometimes this means that you hit a different life stage to a friend and you know, no matter what, she's never going to get to the stage that you're at. This can lead to feelings of guilt and, if left to build up for long enough, resentment. You have that feeling of dread in the pit of your stomach when you have to go and see that friend, and spend the evening watching the clock to see when you can leave without being rude. Wanting to ditch a friend doesn't make you a bad person. After all, it's perfectly accepted that sexual relationships don't all last for ever, so why should a friendship be any different?

The Life Cycle of Friendships

Kathryn's story: I lost the custody battle

I dumped my best friend in high school. We are both named Katie, and so were known as the inseparable Katie one and Katie two. I harbor no resentment that I was number two. Anyway. We had a fabulous friendship up until she moved away for a year and just changed. When she came back she had become entirely self-involved, but I overlooked it for a time.

It was about nine months after she had returned, a changed girl, that I finally became fed up with her. In the course of one week, she blew off our plans together three times. I rather see myself as the most important person in the world, as most people do, but I'll put up with a re-scheduling here and there. This, however, was too much. I realised that I had stopped being the best friend and become the nothing-better-to-do friend. After she cancelled on me the third time, calling from a party she was already at, without me, I called her back and told her I didn't want her to call me any more. She said, 'We'll talk about this later.' And I said, 'No we won't.' And we didn't.

Unfortunately, our break was like a divorce and all our mutual friends were our kids. She won the custody battle because it was high school and she was the only one with a car. I guess they were shallow friends anyway.

Best friends cannot be one-sided, or rely on an 'understanding' of flexibility too much. One friend cannot rely on the other to be there unconditionally. No matter how much they may love each other, if there is less love on one side, the unloved will

You Must Be My Best Friend ...

feel taken advantage of, and either grow depressed and turn into a bad friend, or break the friendship, like I did.

Trying to cling on to a friendship that just isn't working any more can be a sign of insecurity: you're scared that if you ditch this friend, you won't make any more pals. It can also happen because you're afraid of hurting another person: in part, because you're a compassionate human being, and possibly because you feel the need to be a 'people-pleaser' and hate the idea of anyone disliking you so don't want a confrontation. Or it can just be laziness: you keep meaning to tell your friend you don't want to see her but it's easier to just go along with her suggestions of meeting up.

To be blunt, if you don't enjoy spending time with someone then don't do it. Not only are you wasting time in your own life that could be spent doing things that you enjoy, but you're also eating into her social life. She could be spending the time that she's with you hanging out with someone who genuinely enjoys her company, so, in actual fact, you're not being fair to her by chickening out of ditching her.

Tanika's story: She bores me

I'm currently trying to 'lose' a friend, due to outgrowing her. Jenny and I were at school together and, though we lost touch

The Life Cycle of Friendships

for many years, I invited her along with several other school friends to my 30th birthday party.

We're both from very contrasting working environments – I'm in media and she's a legal secretary – but we were both single, so we started going out to parties together. We would have fun, but I started to feel that the friendship was rather one-sided. I would always invite Jen along when there was an event or party and she would happily come along but the invites on her side were decidedly sparse – and when they did come, they weren't my type of thing.

Jen has always been extremely chatty and on our nights out it became increasingly obvious that we only ever talked about her life and she never asked about mine, even though she knew I was doing any number of exciting things relating to my job and hobbies. I could also never get below the superficial level when we talked. I found this very frustrating – this lack of intimacy with someone who had known me for 25 years. After a couple of years I decided there was no point investing precious time on a friendship just out of duty, when all we really had in common was our schooling. So I'm currently attempting to let the relationship slide. I don't email or call, and if she mails me I'm friendly but don't suggest meeting up and don't acknowledge it if she does. It feels cruel but she has plenty of friends she is close to – there is no way she's actually missing me – and she also now has a boyfriend so that should make it even easier.

*

You Must Be My Best Friend ...

So how do you dump someone without pain? As with the end of any relationship, it's not always easy. One of the weakest, but easiest ways is to simply drift apart. Every time your friend calls to meet up, say that you're busy. Don't call her to make any arrangements and don't invite her to any of your social functions. After a while, she should get the hint. However, this is unfair on her, and may make her feel insecure because she's constantly the one making the effort. But it does avoid conflict, and if she hasn't done anything wrong – you've just outgrown the friendship – then it can be the least painful way to deal with things.

The mature but slightly harder way to end a friendship is to be honest – albeit gently. Tell your friend that you're going through a lot of changes right now and you need some time away from old influences to figure out what's going on in your head. Don't make it personal – telling someone they bore you or don't fit with your life any more is just plain mean. By distancing your friend from your decision to stop being friends with her, you're effectively using the old 'it's not you, it's me' line. And that's much easier to deal with than being told you're dull.

If you've had a big row about something then you can tell her that it's something you don't feel that you can get over and it's best if you don't see each other for a while. It's amazing how easy it is to let 'a while' drift into 'for ever'. And, if you're feeling really Machiavellian, you can manufacture a row. However, this is low behaviour so should absolutely be a

The Life Cycle of Friendships

last resort. It's the kind of thing that cowardly blokes do when they're too scared to dump a woman, and you don't really want to end up behaving like a cowardly bloke now, do you?

JM's story: He cut them out of his life

This isn't my story, it's about a friend of mine, who wanted to dump a couple of friends. He travels around a lot, and so he and his friends communicated by postcard and letter. He had an address book, in which they had written their addresses. When he wanted to show that he had dumped them, he cut out the entry from the address book, and glued it to the letter: his way of showing that they weren't going to get another letter from him.

It's also worth bearing in mind that, just because the friendship isn't working for you at the moment, given a bit of time and space, things could get back on track. After all, people do change all the time, and by this time next year you could both be entirely different people. So, as far as possible, avoid burning bridges. That way, you'll be minimising the hurt and potential damage for both of you.

You Must Be My Best Friend ...

Lizzie's story: She broke my trust

A few years ago, I was working with a friend, Rachel, on a project. I'd introduced her to the company running the project, and she was hired on my recommendation even though they'd initially thought that she was under-qualified. We tended to share a lot of responsibilities and it wasn't uncommon for us to both end up working on the same report. As such, we used to send our work to each other so that we could check that we'd both included all the facts.

One day, I got a call from my boss. He was concerned because Rachel's latest report read an awful lot like I'd written it. I asked him to send it over and was shocked to discover that she'd submitted the last report that I'd written with her own name on it. We were paid by the report, so she'd effectively used my work to make herself money. I was horrified and told the boss what had happened. Luckily, he believed me, but because the nature of the project was quite sensitive and we were nearing deadline, he decided to keep us both on anyway.

From that point forward, I couldn't send her any of my work – I knew that I couldn't trust her. I dropped hints to her about sharing work, even going so far as to say that if she was behind on her work, I didn't mind writing a report for her but she said that she couldn't possibly expect me to do that. I was furious that she was so duplicitous.

At the end of the project, she suggested that we went out to celebrate. I said that I was too busy – I couldn't be in the same room as her because I knew that I'd bring it up and there was no way that I wanted to lose my temper with her. I like being quite calm.

That happened two years ago. Now, she'll still occasionally get in contact with me but I ignore her. Part of me feels bad for not confronting her but, to be honest, given that she's lied to me before, I wouldn't be able to accept that she was telling me the truth about anything else. I need to be able to trust my friends and I know that I could never trust Rachel again.

Spotting the signs

Of course, it's not always you that will want to do the dumping. Sometimes, a friend will outgrow you. It doesn't mean that you're a bad person. It simply means that the connection your friend once felt with you is no longer there: one or both of you could have changed over the duration of your friendship. This is normal, natural and, obviously, painful.

Signs that a friend is trying to dump you could include her not answering or returning your phone calls, or suddenly being busy every time that you suggest meeting up. You may start to hear about events that she was at and you weren't invited to. Of course, all of these things could have simple explanations – and you don't know unless you ask her.

Birthdays and other special occasions are a good way of testing this out, if you can wait that long. Suggest taking your friend out for a birthday treat at some stage during her birthday week. If she doesn't even want to go out with you when she's going to get a present, she's probably not all that keen – although, even this can have an innocent explanation though, particularly if she's got a lot of friends or has a busy life.

The most effective way to find out whether someone's trying to dump you is to ask. Ideally, put together an email – the distance makes it easier to be balanced and honest. Don't say, 'Do you hate me?' or use otherwise emotive language. Simply say something like, 'I've noticed that you tend to be busy a lot of the time. I like you and enjoy our friendship but if you're finding it hard to keep in contact with me, then say as I'd rather know.' If she likes you, you'll get a grovelling apology back sharpish, and if you don't get a straight answer, the friendship is no real loss. But whatever the outcome, don't feel bad about asking. If a man was messing you around, you'd ask him what was going on, so why treat a friend any differently?

> NB: It's worth bearing in mind that if a friend starts to avoid you, it could be a sign that there's something more serious going on: drink or drug abuse, mental illness or domestic violence. See chapter six for ways to spot the signs.

The Life Cycle of Friendships

Greta's story: He dumped me for his partner

Karl and I were inseparable. He was my best mate for ten years – through university, my first marriage and my subsequent divorce. I never thought that there would come a time when he wasn't around – he was my best friend in the world. I'd helped him through coming out and he'd helped me through my breakup. We'd spend most weekends together and talk almost every night, even though he hated chatting on the phone to anyone else. And then he met Tariq. I was really pleased to see him in a loving relationship, but Tariq was jealous of me from day one. Whenever Karl was on the phone to me, Tariq would stand next to him and ask how long he was going to be. Tariq even organised a surprise birthday party for Karl and didn't invite me. Karl was in love so didn't say anything about it, which hurt me, particularly given everything that we'd been through.

After a couple of months of this, I decided to talk to Tariq about it and explain that I wasn't a threat. After all, Karl loved Tariq. I was just his best friend – and it wasn't like he was going to run off with me, given that I was the wrong gender!

Tariq and I had what I thought was a really good chat. He explained that he was threatened by the intimacy that Karl and I had, even though it wasn't sexual. He said that he felt left out whenever I was with Karl because we had so much in common. I said that there was no need to feel like that and that I'd never seen Karl so happy with anyone. After that conversation,

I thought everything was sorted. Tariq and I left on good terms so I guessed the problem was solved.

How wrong could I be? Even after our conversation, Tariq kept making digs about me to Karl, and in the end Karl stopped returning my calls. It broke my heart to lose what I thought was such a strong friendship over something so stupid. But after sending birthday and Christmas cards to Karl every year for five years, only to get no response, I gave up. A friendship only works if both people are interested in it and clearly, I was less important to Karl than he was to me.

Dealing with a Friendship Breakup

Of course, getting dumped by a pal isn't something that is always all that easy to shrug off. If a bloke dumps you, it may hurt but you can always blame it on him not fancying you (which stings, but not nearly as much as someone disliking your personality) or put it down to him being a rubbish man. If a friend dumps you, it reflects more on your personality. You may find yourself obsessing over what you did wrong: were you too boring, needy or thoughtless? After all, a friend is supposed to like you for who you are, so when you get rejected, it's far more hurtful an attack.

Added to this, we don't have coping mechanisms in place to deal with the loss of a friend. There's an unwritten rule that, if you get dumped by a man, the way to deal with it is to either

The Life Cycle of Friendships

a) drink a bottle of wine and sob until your face gets all red and blotchy, b) eat excesses of ice cream then panic that the reason you're single is because you're fat, or c) sit around with your friends complaining that all men are bastards (extra points for combining all three activities).

If a friend leaves you, on the other hand, you may feel a bit foolish sitting round and sobbing, and it's unlikely you'll want a bitching session about that friend — even if you do, it may be harder to find people willing to enter into it with the vitriol that a man-bashing session entails.

Try not to get too depressed if a friend dumps you. Just because she doesn't want to stay in contact, it doesn't mean that you're an unlikeable person. To get all Disney on you, it's just part of the 'circle of life'. The best way to deal with it is to look at yourself and see it as a learning experience.

Write down the reason for the breakup (if you know) and consider whether there are any grounds. Sometimes it will purely be down to situation: one or both of you has changed. If so, remind yourself that nobody stays the same throughout their life and if you've drifted apart because you no longer have shared interests or a similar lifestyle, you'll soon attract other people who love you as you are. Added to which, if a change of lifestyle is enough to end the friendship, it was clearly past its sell-by-date and not what you thought it was.

Sometimes a friendship will end because of distance. Give it time. When someone first moves to a new place, they're often lonely and scared so try extra hard to settle in, which can mean

You Must Be My Best Friend ...

neglecting friends back home. Make things easy on your pal — she's probably feeling stressed as it is. If the friendship is worth keeping, you'll end up in contact again once she's properly settled in. And if not, bear in mind that it takes a lot of hard work to maintain a long distance friendship, so at least you're being saved a lot of hassle!

And at other times, a friendship breakdown will be down to an argument. So look at what happened and see if you could take a different perspective. Maybe you'll decide in hindsight that you should concede because your pal was right. Or, after looking at things in more detail, you may still think that, actually, your friend is utterly in the wrong — even though they believe they're right. Unless it's a case of factual misunderstanding, get over it; if you've had a conversation about the issue with your friend, explaining the real story and they still refuse to believe anything other than their own version of events, then they never will. Different people perceive the same events in different ways — like it or not, human beings aren't objective — so you'll only drive yourself insane trying to make them see things the way that you do. And if whatever has come between you is more important to your ex-friend than your friendship, then she can't have been that good a friend in the first place.

Whatever the reason for a friendship failing, analysing why things didn't work out will help you get it into perspective. And even if you can't salvage the ex-friendship, you may learn about negative sides of yourself that you can look at getting rid of.

The Life Cycle of Friendships

Don't be scared to mourn the lost friendship — a good crying session can help relieve stress — but don't obsess over it. Allow yourself no more than a month to actively grieve the loss of a friendship (assuming that it was a long-term friendship — less if you hadn't known the person long). Then move on to other friends. That person didn't like you — well, so what? You've got other friends. And even if not, there are plenty of other people on the planet, and some of them are bound to like you. All you need to do is get out there and meet them.

Christina's story: She broke my heart

I used to have a best friend. She wasn't my oldest friend, but we were bosom buddies for about six years in high school. We had the same sporting hobby and spent a lot of time together, drooling over boys, the way you do when you're 14. I shared all my important moments and hopes and fears with her, and she did the same. She was prettier than me and there were always guys interested in her. I admired her with a kind of benign envy.

When the time came, we both went off to our respective universities. She made friends, I made other friends, but we still saw each other, though less frequently. We both did well at university, and graduated, and then wondered what to do next. She started doing a PhD, then quit suddenly, deciding it wasn't what she wanted. I got a job, not wanting to commit to postgraduate study straight away, but thinking I might come back to it. She did

You Must Be My Best Friend ...

all sorts of jobs – make-up counter assistant, lab scientist, cabin crew for a local airline. I admired the way she could make a living doing anything (I'm kind of bookish – I was always going to be stuck with geeky jobs).

I moved further from home to start a PhD and live with my boyfriend. I saw her less, but I was still very fond of her. In a rare phone call, she mentioned that she and her boyfriend had decided, a few months ago, to get married in a couple of years. They hadn't wanted to make a big deal out of it to anyone, even family. I was disappointed she hadn't told me sooner; I suppose she could probably tell.

Not long after that, my boyfriend and I were in town and visited them. We took a bottle of champagne to celebrate the engagement. They put it to one side. We then proceeded to have the absolutely most awkward evening ever. It started out OK but then we got into a discussion on gay rights, something my then-boyfriend and I were, and still are, very passionately in favour of. Her argument (she graduated in a biology-related subject) was that it was a biological irrelevance, and because gay sex wasn't procreative it didn't serve any purpose, so there was no point in protecting gay relationships. Sometime soon after that, we made our excuses and left.

I was fuming for days afterwards – months, even. You think you know someone! It festered at the back of my mind for ages, until I decided I'd had enough, and wrote her a letter to say that I felt terrible that the evening had gone badly, and that although

The Life Cycle of Friendships

I disagreed with her about gay rights, she was entitled to her opinion. I said I was sorry that we had drifted out of touch because I still felt really warmly towards her and missed her company. I think I said that I still thought she was terrific.

At that point, my mum died suddenly. When I came back from sorting everything out at home, there was a letter from my friend. It all came pouring out. Her family had made her feel bad about not telling them for ages that she had got engaged, and some of the bad feeling had come out at me. She said it was ridiculous to bother about gay rights when there were people in Tibet being killed for their beliefs. She went off on a rant about how she and her boyfriend hardly drank, and they didn't go out to pubs, and when they did they were just quiet little country ones. She said she didn't think my boyfriend and I did anything apart from going out and drinking (conveniently overlooking all the sport we did and music we played, and the intellectual pursuits), and that a life like that wasn't worth anything. She spat my compliments about being terrific right back at me, saying she felt I'd always looked down on her, particularly when she was with the airline (she said that I always made her feel like she was my 'novelty friend'). She said she always felt, around me, that she wasn't bright or academic enough (this from the woman who got a first at university, whereas I only got a 2:1). She said she couldn't really be friends with me any more because she didn't feel that we had anything in common, but that she'd be there for me if I ever needed someone to talk to. As if, after all that!

I never wrote, or called her, again. I didn't tell her my mum had died. I never heard whether she got married (I assume she did). After I'd simmered down (it took a few months) I read her letter again and realised that there was absolutely nothing I could say, or write, that would do anything other than confirm her prejudices about me.

I've still got the letter and it still makes me incredibly bitter. She was one of those friends who you think you'll have your whole life, and it absolutely broke my heart that she decided there was 'no point' being friends any more because of a few differences in outlook, and that she had spent years and years feeling inferior to me when I had only ever looked up to and admired her! Those differences are what make life interesting. I've never had a breakup in a relationship that affected me like breaking up with my best friend.

MAKING NEW FRIENDS

Most of us are happy with the amount of friends we have, but it's not uncommon to go through periods in life where we would like a few more friends. Indeed, according to queendom.com, 10 per cent of people would currently like more friends in their life. Without friends, we're likely to feel isolated or lonely.

The causes of loneliness are varied. There are only so many hours in the day, and maintaining friendships takes time – you

The Life Cycle of Friendships

might feel that good friendships have just slipped away, or realise too late that you've neglected friends and they've moved on. Or you might end up feeling like you have a gap in your life left from either dumping a friend or being dumped by one, moving to a new town, going travelling or ending a relationship (alternatively, you might decide that this is a good thing — it gives you more time to spend with the rest of your friends, so you can make more of an effort with them).

If you decide that you need to find another friend (or a whole group of people), you might feel embarrassed about it. After all, people don't exactly go 'on the pull' for pals. But a few tricks will make it a lot easier for you to make new friends if one or more drop out of your life, or if you simply feel lonely.

It's worth bearing in mind that feeling lonely isn't always down to the amount of friends you have, but the quality of the friendships. You could have endless friends that you could go shopping and partying with but no one to talk to about your favourite books, or to have a heart to heart with. Depending on whether this is something that's always been the case, or if you're just going through a ropey patch, you may want to get counselling to help you attract more like-minded people, or learn how to open up more with friends. Otherwise, you may find yourself becoming insular and rejecting the entire notion of friendship. This can have knock-on effects to your self-esteem.

You Must Be My Best Friend ...

A note about counselling

Don't feel bad if you end up seeking counselling. Friends can't help you sort out every problem you encounter, and neither should you expect them to. That's not to say that you shouldn't turn to friends for help, or try to work through problems — like shyness or feelings of isolation — on your own, but it's often more useful in the long run to find professional help for serious and/or underlying issues. It also saves you from overburdening your friends.

If you're facing conflict with friends that you're unable to resolve, don't be scared of working through problems in group therapy or with a counsellor. One word of warning though: a therapist can feel like a best friend, but that doesn't mean they are your friend — they're doing a job. However, they have the professional skills to give you the correct advice and to be able to handle however much you need to tell them.

Laura's story: I don't have friends

First, me: Female, recently remarried after long and horrible 20-year confinement, which produced four of the most brilliant

The Life Cycle of Friendships

and attractive children ever. 45 years old. No current friends. Absolutely none.

I had two very good friends in high school and we did lots of fun things together, such as follow cute guys home from school, shoplift large amounts of candy and other junk foods from convenience stores, and make lewd snow people in the front yard at midnight.

Then, I moved away and got married, then had a baby before I was 21 years old. I had moved into a new sphere and left them sitting on barstools getting sloppy drunk, while I was home watching *Sesame Street* and leaking milk from my breasts.

In the ensuing 23 years I have not made one single adult friend. It seems like too much work and I have been totally centred on being a mother and feel I am much too boring and my world too small to be an interesting friend to someone.

I see small groups of women talking in the grocery store, or two best friends walking arm in arm and I feel a very deep longing to have that again. But I just don't know how.

No matter how boring you may feel, you can guarantee that there are other people who will connect with you — you just need to meet them. In Laura's case, her experience as a mother could prove invaluable at a mother and baby group; or she could get chatting to someone over grocery coupons. And listening is an essential part of friendship, so even if she doesn't feel she has anything exciting to talk about, she could be a wonderful friend. Making friends is easy: you just need to know a few tricks.

Use your brain

It doesn't take a rocket scientist to figure out that you're more likely to make friends if you get out of your house and do things that bring you into contact with other people. However, unlike landing a shag, you can't just walk up to someone in a bar and suddenly make new friends (or at least, it's unlikely). Friendships develop naturally and aren't really things that can be contrived – you can't really 'chat up' friends. That said, you can put yourself in the situation where you can meet plenty of people, and you can be more courageous with chatting to people you don't know.

If you frequent a local bar or pub and talk to the same group of people who also go to the same bar/pub, a friendship might easily develop. Although you shouldn't go *too* far out of your way to talk to people (it should be natural), otherwise you may come across as a bit of a stalker!

One useful tip is to always take a book to read if you go out alone. Should you hear something that interests you, don't be scared to pipe up with a: 'I'm sorry but I couldn't help overhearing you talk about that new exhibition in town. I went last week and it's amazing,' or similar, as this will help you initiate contact. If your conversation doesn't seem welcome, go

The Life Cycle of Friendships

straight back to reading your book as this shows that you're not phased or clingy.

However, a much easier idea is to make a list of everything that you enjoy doing: going to the cinema, visiting an art gallery, spending a day by the sea or whatever. Then make a list of everyone you know – be that colleagues, neighbours or that girl who serves you coffee every morning on your way to work – and try to match them to the activities you think they'd enjoy. All you need to do then is ask if they'd like to join you – you can always say you have a spare ticket if you're nervous about making the approach – and *voilà*, a potential friendship is born.

You can also go for the night school route – and don't think it has to be boring. Nowadays, you can take classes in pole dancing and striptease, alongside more traditional things like car maintenance or reading groups. If you pick a course that reflects your interests, you're more likely to meet similar people – and you can talk about the class so you've already got something in common. Try to pick an ongoing course rather than a single term evening class as this gives you more scope for developing friendships. Joining a sports club, campaigning group or volunteering for charity all work in similar ways. And the advantage of them all is that you're doing something that you enjoy, so you won't feel lonely or desperate. Added to which, happy people are more attractive as friends, so you're in an ideal situation.

Another great way to meet people is through the internet. Join a newsgroup or bulletin board for like-minded people. A

You Must Be My Best Friend...

quick internet search (in the 'groups' category) will throw up more niche interests than you could possibly imagine, so you're bound to find people who love cooking, Andalucian artwork or Frank Zappa just as much as you do. And there are groups out there for new mums, feminists, vegans and every other kind of person. So hit the net. Some of these friendships may stay purely online but others can convert into 'real life' friendships — and either way, a new friend is a good thing. You can still talk about your problems over email or instant messenger, even if you never meet face-to-face (indeed, internet relationships often have a particular intimacy because it can get rid of barriers and retains a slightly 'anonymous' quality).

However, most friends that you make are likely to be face to face — which is why it's important knowing how to present yourself in the right light.

Use your body

According to research by Nalani Ambady at the Harvard University Department of Psychology, it takes only ten seconds to form a first impression. So, if you're going to attract new friends, you need to make sure that your first impression is a good one, and that means ensuring you're in control of every aspect of your presentation. Being well groomed and sweet smelling (come on, who wants a stinky mate?) is only one part of it. A whopping 55 per cent of communication is down to your body language, so make sure that you have open body posture, showing that you're willing to be approached. Keep your arms and legs uncrossed, and avoid 'blocking' someone, by putting a table or anything else between you.

It may sound obvious but, when you're out and about in 'friend-hunting' mode, the most important thing is to make sure that you smile. A smile is one of the few universal pieces of body language. It makes you seem more approachable to both prospective friends and partners, which is a great double-whammy.

It's not what you say, it's the way that you say it

Once you've got your body language sorted, you're not off the hook. You need to pay attention to the way that you speak too. 38 per cent of communication is down to tone of voice so make sure that yours shows you'd be a great addition to anyone's friendship circle. Generally speaking, people prefer low voices to shrill ones. Your voice should be easy to hear without being too loud. Pay attention to your diction; pronouncing words clearly makes it a lot easier for someone to understand what you're saying. And don't speak too fast, or too slowly. If you go with the former, people can miss what you say, while the latter could leave them tapping their fingers impatiently waiting for you to finish your sentence.

You Must Be My Best Friend ...

It may sound excessive, but if you have a nasal or grating voice, it's worth investing in some voice training — otherwise, you could be alienating potential friends before you get a chance to know them. And let your smile come through in your voice. Try this on the phone when calling a new friend: plaster a broad grin on your face as you talk and it really will make a difference to the way that you sound — even if you do feel like a total idiot while you're doing it. (NB: doing this in a shared office or flat is probably not a good idea.)

Talking the talk

All that messing around with your tone of voice might sound like hard work, but the good news is that only 7 per cent of people's impression of you is down what you actually say so if you do embarrass yourself by making a stupid comment when you meet someone new, you can rest assured that it won't matter all that much unless your body language and tone of voice were also negative. See, being control of your body does have some benefits.

However, when you're first meeting someone new, it's best to hold back any particularly controversial views that you have, and save that discussion for a time when you know that person better. Few things are more embarrassing than spending ten minutes venting your loathing of a particular pop star or politician, only to find out that the person you're talking to is a massive fan of the band, or related to the politician. You might get lucky and manage to salvage things by saying, 'I was

The Life Cycle of Friendships

playing devil's advocate – I can't believe you fell for it,' but it's more likely that the person concerned will just decide they don't like you. On similar lines, sexist, racist, homophobic or otherwise negative views are not the kind of thing that's likely to endear you to a stranger so if you do have any then keep them to yourself. (Come on, would you really want to be friends with a sexist, racist homophobe?)

One of the best ways to start a conversation with someone is by giving them a (genuine) compliment or commenting on some kind of shared ground – for example, the venue that you're in – rather than to wading in with opinion. Look for any clues that the person is similar to you: maybe they're wearing a T-shirt with a band you like on it, or have a book poking out of their bag that you've read. Like really does attract like – so look for the similarities between yourself and another person and they're more likely to see you as someone they'd like to know better. And ask them questions about themselves too. Most people love talking about themselves and they won't notice that they're doing the bulk of the talking – they'll just remember you as a really interesting person because people like others who are interested in them.

But even when you're immersed in conversation, keep your body language under control. If there's a contradiction between your words and your body language, people will take your body language as the most accurate sign of your intent – so if you say, 'I'm having a great time chatting to you – can we hook up some time?' while your posture is defensive and you're unsmiling, then you're shooting your attempts to make a new friend in the foot. They'll put you down as being untrustworthy or after something from them instead.

By following these guidelines, you should find it easier to meet new people and get new additions to your social circle. But if you've gone out and met a load of people and the phone still isn't ringing off the hook from them calling to invite you out, don't panic. It takes time to establish a friendship, just as it does with relationships. Chances are, if you haven't heard from a potential new friend, it's not that they disliked you – they just haven't had time to call. So don't be scared make the first move. In fact, why wait at all? Call someone you like the day after you've met them (not to early in the morning or you might seem scary) and they'll see you as organised as well as realising that you like them, so you'll get double brownie-points. After all, one phone call is very little effort to put in if you end up making a great new friend.

THE TEN COMMANDMENTS FOR MAKING NEW FRIENDS

1. Like yourself. If you don't, why should anybody else?
2. Smile at people. It will make them feel all warm inside and make you seem more approachable.
3. Make sure your body language tallies with what you're saying.

The Life Cycle of Friendships

4. Look everywhere for new friends: night classes, campaign groups or even the internet. And get your friends to introduce you to their friends – there's a strong chance that you'll get on with them, particularly if you're similar to your friend.
5. Establish areas of common ground as soon as possible. People like others who are similar. (NB: the only similarity that may not lead to friendship is having both dated the same person – particularly if it was at the same time …)
6. If you've got nothing to say, listen instead. People will think you're interesting because most people love the sound of their own voice. Just make affirmations (nodding your head, or saying, 'yes, go on,') during conversation so that the person doesn't feel they're delivering a monologue.
7. Don't get too personal when you first meet someone; talking about your love of tennis is fine. Talking about your love of big cock, even though the last time you had someone who was hung like a donkey it gave you cystitis, isn't.
8. Having a glass of wine or pint of beer is fine, if you need Dutch courage to approach a potential friend, but don't get drunk or you'll give the wrong impression.
9. Don't take cruel comments to heart. If a stranger is mean to you, it says more about them than it does about you.
10. Get out there to meet people – and if you meet someone and get on with them, don't be scared to make that call to organise meeting up again. Someone has to make the first move, after all.

Chapter Three

Unequal Friendships

So, you know what makes a good friend. You've surrounded yourself with people that you like, and got rid of anyone that you don't like. Sorted? No. You could still find yourself in the situation where you feel taken for granted, get jealous of a friend's success or always end up doing what your friend wants and getting resentful, even though you love that friend to bits. Yes, welcome to the world of unequal friendships.

As with any relationship, it's not uncommon for friendships to be slightly skewed to one person's advantage: one person makes the bulk of the effort in the friendship, grateful to be their friend, while the other sits back 'accepting' the friendship but putting very little in.

Sadly, it's not always that easy to spot. Inequality in friendships is very rarely a clear-cut situation. However, going through a mental checklist will help you establish whether any of your friendships are unbalanced. Once you've identified the problem, it's easy enough to sort, after all.

You Must Be My Best Friend ...

THE INEQUALITY CHECKLIST

To find out whether there's enough give and take in your friendship, ask yourself the following questions:

Do you make the bulk of the phone calls?

When it comes to catching up with friends, ideally, there should be two-way traffic: sometimes you call them, sometimes they call you. However, the reality is very different. Some people love talking on the phone while others will be phone-phobic and do almost anything to avoid it.

Phone phobia is particularly common among men, because they talk less than women do. According to *Why men listen and women can't read maps* by Allan and Barbara Peas, the female brain can easily process 6,000–8,000 words per day, while men's maximum output is 4,000 words per day. So, by the time a bloke finishes his working day, he's used up most of his words, whereas a woman is more likely to have words to spare on a long conversation with a friend. There are various solutions: text to arrange meeting up face-to-face (you can talk while he listens, as face-to-face there's less pressure for the conversation to be equally divided between you) or use email or instant messenger to catch up instead. The most phone-phobic pal will probably be more than willing to exchange long emails so you can still keep up with what's going on in each other's lives between seeing each other.

You also need to take money into account: if you're loaded and your mate's broke, she may not be able to afford hours chatting on the phone. Again, email or instant messenger (assuming broadband access) can be a solution. Alternatively, you could buy her a pay-as-you-go phone for her birthday, with phone cards to charge it up – but be careful that this doesn't backfire. If she wants to chat but can't afford it, she may feel guilty and one guaranteed way to get someone's back up and make them feel insecure is to play up to their guilt.

The problem of imbalance comes in if you make the bulk of the phone calls and your friend is off-hand with you. If she promises she'll call back but never does or somehow never gets round to meeting up with you even though you've chatted about it, prepare yourself mentally for the idea that she may be trying to drop hints she doesn't want to be in contact as much as you do. You may see her as being in your 'inner-circle' of friends whereas she may see you as more of a casual pal. Decide whether this is enough for you, and if it is, lighten up and stop expecting any more from her. If not, move on and find a friend who's prepared to make as much effort as you are.

Carrie's story: She thought I was too much

Angela and I got to know each other relatively quickly: we met at a party, got on like old friends instantly and were soon having

You Must Be My Best Friend ...

lengthy discussions on the phone most days. Our conversation tended to revolve around both of our terrible love lives, and I frequently found myself giving her advice.

After we'd known each other for a couple of months, I hit a particularly bad patch. I'm a depressive and a lot of things had all gone wrong at the same time, so it had brought my symptoms to the fore. My first thought was to call Angela; after all, I'd given her loads of advice and I really needed something to help drag me out of the hole I was in.

I called her for a chat and was clearly very upset. She listened, and made all the right noises. I felt much better after we talked. The next day, something else awful happened and I called her, but she was really short with me, and said she didn't have time for long phone conversations any more because she had a lot of things going on in her life. I felt betrayed: I'd listened to all of her problems and felt that, now I needed help, she'd turned her back on me. I decided that she didn't really like me and so stopped calling her entirely.

About a week later, she gave me a call to talk about her latest crisis. I listened, gave her some advice, but about half way through the conversation felt like I had to ask what was going on. I explained that I'd felt hurt at her behaviour, and she said that she was feeling mentally drained at the moment, so didn't have time to be an emotional support: she needed time to sort her own head out.

Even though part of me felt that it was a bit one-sided, I could understand where she was coming from. I realised that I'd been using her as a surrogate partner – someone to offload everything on to – and that that was too much to expect from one person. I backed off and the friendship got stronger again, though with much less contact than before, and a lot less strong that it had originally been because I no longer fully trusted her.

I still feel reticent about calling her in case it's at a time that's not good for her, and it definitely changed the way I perceived the friendship, but she's still someone I value in my life. I now know that I shouldn't be so demanding of one friend in future – at least not until I know for certain that they see the friendship in the same way as I do. And I know that friendships can seem very different from one person to another. I thought she was my new best friend, but she just saw me as an acquaintance.

Do you take charge of most social arrangements?

While it may seem unfair if you end up making all the social arrangements and can be a sign of an imbalanced friendship, it's not always that simple. Some people are organised, and others aren't. No matter how unfair it seems if you're the organised one, it ain't going to change. Just because you make all the social arrangements, it doesn't mean that your friend isn't prepared to put in any effort – she's might just be incapable of organising herself. Anyway, being the 'organised one' can sometimes be a good thing. After all, if you're making the arrangements, it means you get to decide where you're going, when, and with whom. But if you think that you might have fallen into this trap, ask your friend to pick somewhere for you to go together. She might think that you're entirely happy arranging things — or she may even be desperate to have a chance to be the 'organised one' herself.

If, however, you end up making the arrangements and your friend cancels at the last minute, or complains the entire time she's there, you could be trapped in negative patterns. Don't feel that you have to put everything on a plate for a friend in order for them to like you. A real friend will be just as happy chilling out with you at your flat as she will be going somewhere exciting — and she'll be willing to work at the friendship just as much as you do.

Cassie's story: I turned into her PA, not her friend

Jenny and I met at school. She was almost a year younger than me - my birthday's in September and hers is in August so we were in the same school year - and I always felt a bit protective towards her. We spent most of our time together, as you do when you're a kid. As we got older, we went to the same college and university. We even lived in the same hall of residence.

I began to notice, when we got to university, that Jenny always relied on me to make arrangements for the pair of us: if

I got invited to a party, she'd expect me to take her with me, and whenever I went home for the weekend, she'd just spend her time in her room, alone. It's not as if she's that shy - she gets on with new people really easily. I soon realised that she was too lazy to sort her own life out.

Her dependency began to show in other ways too: she was always running out of money and asking to borrow some from me, even though we were both on student grants and I hadn't got enough money to pay my own way, let alone anyone else's. She 'borrowed' my food and never replaced it. When she started chasing the same man I'd been lusting after all term, I decided enough was enough. We had a massive row and I told her that she needed to get her own life and stop expecting me to deal with everything or live her life for her. She accused me of being a control freak, which was totally unfair. I didn't speak to her after that, even when we were in the shared kitchen together. The next year, I moved out of halls, and away from having her in my life at all. I don't regret it at all.

Do you pay your fair share?

Money is a contentious issue at the best of times — the old adage 'never a borrower or a lender be' is a good one to bear in mind when it comes to friendship. That way, you can avoid feeling resentful if you've paid for the last three nights out and your friend still hasn't paid you back — or avoid feeling guilty if you owe your pal for nights out but can't afford to give them the money because your bank balance is redder than your face gets when you realise you've left the loo with your skirt tucked into your knickers. Instead, make sure that you each pay your fair share, rather than sponging from your pals, or acting as their financial cushion.

The problem comes when you have friends with different income levels. A rich friend might want to go for a night at the latest celebrity hot spot, spending a fortune on cocktails with prices that suggest they're made from liquid gold, whereas a poorer friend can barely afford a night out at a budget restaurant. The logical thing would seem to be going for nights out that everyone in your friendship circle can afford, but this can lead to resentment from the richer friends who feel like they're not getting to live the lifestyle to match their pay packet.

The best way to get round this problem is with compromise. Let's say you can't afford to spend a night out on cocktails: instead, arrange a cocktail party at home, where everyone brings a bottle. Get everyone to dress up and make some canapés yourself if you really want to push the boat out. That way, you get most of the glamour at a fraction of the price you'd pay in a bar – and you'll probably have more fun without having to deal with evil bouncers and chinless wonders attempting to come on to you all night.

It's also worth sitting down with your friends and explaining that you can't afford expensive nights out, even though you'd love to. You can show willing and make an effort by

Unequal Friendships

budgeting: having one flash night out each month by forgoing your daily cappuccino on the way to work, or making your own packed lunch. If your friends see that you're making an effort, they'll be more likely to plan purse-saving nights out too. And there are benefits to having friends that are richer than you: after all, more money often means a more expensive wardrobe, and if you ask nicely, she might let you borrow her gorgeous clothes.

If you're the richer friend, be sensitive about it. Just because your friend can't afford expensive nights out, it doesn't mean that she has to cramp your style. There are plenty of fun ways to spend time together that don't cost a fortune: visiting art galleries, going for walks in the countryside or taking salsa lessons together. Get creative about the things that you do and, not only will you be helping out your pal but you'll also have a more interesting life packed with exciting activities.

Of course, if you're seriously loaded you can always treat your friends, but be careful that this doesn't leave her feeling beholden or you feeling resentful. It's best to save the generosity for times when it's a big deal – birthdays, say, or a particularly special New Year's night out – rather than falling into the habit of paying her way whenever you go out because you can afford it. Money has a strange tendency to lead to rows so it has to be handled with care.

You Must Be My Best Friend ...

Elaine's story: he treated me like a wallet

When Andrew and I met, we hit it off instantly. He's got a child-like sense of humour that really appeals to me, and it felt like I was reliving my student days by hanging out with him. Don't get me wrong – he could have an intelligent conversation, but it was his sense of fun that really appealed.

Andrew's a freelance photographer, which means that he doesn't have regular work, whereas I work for a bank, so I've got a steady income. As such, whenever we went out, I found myself settling the bill. I can easily afford it so it wasn't that big a deal. I also get invited to lots of corporate events with free champagne, and got into the habit of inviting him along as my guest – I'm single at the moment and that's not something they tend to approve of at work, so having a friend who'd play 'token boyfriend' was handy.

The problem came when I was recently taken ill. I texted him to let him know, and didn't hear anything back. I tried calling him but it went straight through to voicemail. I didn't hear from him for over a week, by which time I was really upset. But not nearly as upset as when I found out why it was that he'd eventually called. He wasn't interested in whether I was feeling better. Instead, he noticed that he'd pencilled a big corporate event I'd invited him to in his diary and wanted to check that it was still on. That was the point that I realised he just saw me as a meal ticket: someone to foot the bill and take him to events that he wouldn't get into otherwise. Even when I told him that I was ill so wouldn't be going, he

Unequal Friendships

didn't ask how I felt – instead he asked if he could have my ticket so that he could take a friend. I was horrified and cut him off my friendship list from that day forward. He may be good fun but he's no friend, and life's too short to support spongers.

And do you feel supported by your friend?

Friendship is about mutual support: if you're always lending a listening ear to a friend but find that it's not reciprocated when you're going through personal problems, it may be that you've got an imbalanced friendship. But it's not always that simple. Some people have lives that are filled with crises while others seem to have a charmed life. If you're one of the former and your friend fits into the latter category, they may find it hard to cope with your incessant demands.

Similarly, if you keep making the same mistakes again and again – dating men who are bad for you, or letting yourself get taken for granted – but ignore your friend's advice, they may give up on supporting you because it's a lot of work for little reward. OK, a good friend will offer advice without expecting you to follow it, but if you make them pick up the pieces every time you go against their advice and make the same mistakes again, you can see how it would get irritating.

As a general guide, people frequently fit into one of three categories: parent, child and adult. The 'parent' has a need to nurture and look after people, the 'child' refuses to take responsibility for their own actions — only the 'adult' relates to people in what could be considered a 'mature' way. This has a massive impact on friendship: people with a need to 'parent' are often drawn to people they can look after — those who have a strong 'child' mask in place. While this may seem like a mutually beneficial relationship, it actually stops either person developing as an 'adult'. In addition, the 'parent' may feel constantly put upon, while the 'child' feels patronised.

Breaking this cycle can be difficult, not to mention painful. The 'parent' needs to let go of the control that they have and let the 'child' make mistakes. In the short-term this may seem damaging, but in the long-term it means that both 'child' and 'parent' have a chance to develop a more fulfilling 'adult' relationship, unlike the story below.

Stephanie's story: I feel like a parent

I was at a party with a bunch of my friends where, of course, alcohol was consumed like bottled water by some of them. I happened to look over towards the end to see my friend, who was in a relationship, about to leave with a reputed man-slut, or whatever you'd like to call it. I told her to come to the bathroom with me and asked her what she was doing. Finally she agreed to go down to her car where I had to sit and wait for her boyfriend to come pick her up while she thanked me over and over again for saving her relationship.

Unequal Friendships

At another point, also involving a party with ample alcohol, I saw my friend's little sister and one of her buddies. I was happy to see them, as I'm quite good friends with her too. I went to the party planning to have fun and say goodbye to my friend who was leaving to fight overseas. I then realised how much my friend's sister and her friend had had to drink, so what I actually did at the party was spend the next two hours walking them around, making them drink water, and getting one of them away from an uncouth excuse for a man who proposed to 'take care of' and 'watch' my friend's sister - a feeble excuse because by guaranteeing to protect her from everyone else he thought, in his own inebriation, that meant he could have her.

Sometimes a friendship may feel imbalanced because you have excessive demands, or are oversensitive. If you find yourself describing the way you've been 'maltreated' by a friend to your other friends, and they look at you blankly, trying to see what your problem is, consider whether you're expecting too much. Friendship is supposed to be about enjoying spending time with someone, not a series of checks, balances and traded favours. If you find yourself keeping score of every nice thing you do, and every negative thing your friend does then chill out and stop being such hard work. Otherwise, you'll find yourself without that friend soon enough.

You Must Be My Best Friend ...

Beth's story: Martyrdom makes people blind

I have always found the most imbalanced friendships are usually with those people who think of themselves as giving everything. Their martyrdom makes them blind to their own selfishness. I had a flatmate – who I am now no longer even mates with – who was like this. Before moving in with me, she lived with a mutual friend who was a single mum and strapped for cash. My flatmate-to-be used to buy things like Marks and Spencer's coffee cake and bottles of wine for them both, and so she was most put out when our friend asked her to buy some milk. She didn't realise that a single mum without much money has a lot more need for milk than all these other luxuries she never asked for.

I was soon to find out this was her attitude to friendship all over. She would take pleasure in doing something unnecessary you never even wanted her to do, then act as though you were indebted to her to make you feel guilty. It was as if every favour was stored up on a list somewhere and not given for nothing. She was the only friend who would ring up and demand that I leave work early to help her do something, or regularly phone in tears and need hours of consoling, but I actually didn't find her nearly so generous with her time when it came to listening to my problems.

I think the best friends are people who don't make huge demands, or consider you indebted to them for their help. I wouldn't think twice about helping a friend but I would also never demand their time. You can only ask.

Unequal Friendships

DEALING WITH CLINGY FRIENDS

All you need to do is watch the film *Single White Female* to see how disturbing having a clingy friend can be. Of course, most clingy friends don't turn psycho and try to stab people in the head with a stiletto, but it can still be a royal pain in the arse.

Clinginess takes many forms: it could be that your friend is incapable of making a life decision without you holding her hand. If this is the case, tell your friend calmly but firmly that you can't be there for her all the time — she needs to make decisions for herself, although you're more than happy to help if you can. Chances are, she's just scared of doing the wrong thing and thinks that following her own gut instinct will lead to trouble, so reassure her that she is good at making decisions — use examples if you can — and she'll be more likely to start taking control of herself. After all, we all have one life, so if she wants you to run hers for you, that means you've got two lives to manage and no one has enough hours in the day to do that.

Alternatively — or in addition to asking you to run her life — your friend might insist on going everywhere with you. Seeing friends is all well and good but spending all your time with any one person is bound to drive you up the wall, no matter how much you like them. It may be that you're the only person she sees as a friend, in which case, take her out and

You Must Be My Best Friend ...

introduce her to more people, encouraging her to make new friends. Explain that you're not trying to palm her off – you love her company – but you need time alone, and time seeing other friends too.

She might hate being alone – many people do – so try introducing her to reading, yoga, computer games or other solitary activities that can fill her time. Everyone should spend some time alone to help them keep a balanced view on life, and needing constant company is an unhealthy trait that you can help her overcome. She'll be grateful in the long run.

Joan's story: He won't give me space

I'm quite a confident person – I never have a problem going up to strangers and getting chatting to them, or making new friends. My friend, Kenny, is much quieter. He's fantastic company when we're on our own together but the second that we're in a social situation he clams up. I end up having to drag conversation out of him, or introduce him to people all night explaining what it is that I think they have in common. I wouldn't mind but the second I stop spoon-feeding him with conversation, he sits in a corner on his own looking sad. I feel guilty if I'm chatting to someone else, and I've lost track of the amount of evenings that I've curtailed early, just because Kenny looks so uncomfortable.

I suggested to him that we only meet up when we're alone, as he doesn't like the social whirl, but he says that he likes going out with me to parties, and that he enjoys meeting new people through me. It's beginning to ruin my social life having to baby-sit him all the time, and I've even resorted to lying about what I'm doing so that he doesn't come along. I feel like a bad friend, but it's the only way I can think of to deal with the situation because he refuses to make an effort in any other way.

Another form of clinginess is copying a friend. On the one hand, finding your friend copies you can be a bit of a compliment: she clearly respects your opinion/life/wardrobe or she wouldn't want it for herself. However, it gets irritating when you go to your third party in as many weeks to find her wearing exactly the same as you.

Surprise, surprise, the root of this problem is down to insecurity. Your friend doesn't feel comfortable enough in her own skin, so is trying yours on for size because she perceives you as being prettier/more successful/generally better than her. Rather than having a go at her when she copies you, make a point of complimenting her when she does something independent, be that going somewhere you've never been or wearing something you'd never wear. By reassuring her that she's a great person, she'll be less likely to want to become you.

Bear in mind, too, that copycat behaviour isn't always intentional. Groups of women often dress alike – particularly if they follow fashion – and many scientists claim that humans tend to mimic the behaviour of each other. Sometimes this is done to show belonging and mark out a group, and at other times on a subconscious level. It can even be down to opportunity: if you live in a small town with only one decent clothes shop, it won't be uncommon for you to end up in the same stuff as your mates (if that is the case, a shopping trip to a nearby city or larger town should sort you out). Whatever the reason, mention it jokingly to your mate: they might be as horrified as you when they realise what they're doing.

Of course, emulating a friend's behaviour can also be a sign of respect. Sometimes, a friend may take on similar hobbies or political views to you because you've inspired them — maybe they start going all 'green' or organic after you do, or decide to join the same gym, sports club or evening class. If you value having a life that's separate from your pals and feel like they're treading on your toes, just tell them. They shouldn't be too offended if you phrase it diplomatically. But surely your life's passions are broad enough to share, and recruiting another member to 'the cause' is only a good thing?

And if you're the one who ends up copying your friend's behaviour remind yourself that you are fantastic in your own right. If you're really insecure, it may be worth getting some counselling to help you work out your issues. Copying a friend is likely to drive a wedge between you. And your pal wouldn't like you if she hadn't thought you were already cool — so just be yourself and you'll have a much more successful friendship.

Unequal Friendships

THE GREEN-EYED MONSTER

And then there's the other problem that can arise from imbalance — that of jealousy. Though the friendship might be perfectly balanced, one person may feel resentful because they feel their friend is superior to them in some way, and get jealous as a result. Common causes of jealousy include 'Pretty mate/ugly mate' syndrome, when you're convinced that your friend is much better looking than you and/or she's always the one to pull when you go out; career jealousy, particularly if you're in similar fields; and financial jealousy, when your friend can afford designer labels while you can't even afford a shopping spree at your local charity shop.

When jealousy rears its head, it can make one person attack another for utterly unfair reasons. A conversation about where to go on Saturday night can spiral into: 'You're so fake, you only ever want to go places where you can get dressed up,' — even though the real meaning behind what's been said is, 'I'm jealous that you can afford to buy the latest designer outfits.'

If you're the one feeling jealous, remember that the grass is always greener. Sure, your friend may have a more glamorous job and better wardrobe than you, but you've got good points too: maybe you have a supportive family, great relationship or are fabulously skilled at cooking — things that your friend is probably secretly jealous about!

You Must Be My Best Friend ...

The best way to deal with feeling jealous is to have it out with your mate. Confess to her that you feel jealous of what she's got, while at the same time explaining that you're happy for her. (If you're not even remotely happy for her can you really consider yourself her friend?) Chances are, she'll admit that she's jealous of you for other reasons, but even if she doesn't, by broaching the subject it means that she'll try to be more sensitive around you. If it's her relationship that you're jealous of, she'll cut down on the amount of 'wedded bliss' stories she tells you, and if it's her sense of style, she might offer to share her wardrobe or at least give you some pointers. Jealousy is most damaging when it's left to fester, so if you open up about it, you'll deal with it in the quickest and most effective way.

If you're the one who's been attacked by an envious friend, remember that most of the time jealousy is down to insecurity. Your friend feels somehow lesser than you and, as such, needs to bring you down to her level by making you feel bad about yourself. Of course, it's not that clinical: your pal may be utterly unaware that this is what she's doing. But if you help boost your friend's confidence rather than automatically getting defensive, it's more likely to get the problem sorted. If she hasn't admitted she's jealous but you can see that she's been bitchy for that reason, it can be tricky to broach the subject. The best bet is to start trying to boost her confidence for a month or so to see if that changes her behaviour. If she's still being a nightmare, lightly pick her up on it when she says

Unequal Friendships

something mean: 'Darling, you don't have to pick on me,' or similar.

Avoid situations that are likely to encourage her jealousy: for example, if she's always nasty when you go on the pull together because you're more successful with men than she is, then don't go on the pull with her. Alternatively, take 'buffer friends' with you so that she's got other people to talk to (as long as they're not bitchy too or you'll spend all night worrying about what they're saying).

Similarly, if she thinks you've got a better body than her, don't go to the beach, swimming or shopping with her – it will only encourage her neurosis. And don't brag about your achievements if it's your success that makes her mean. It may be perfectly natural for you to gush about your new promotion and pay rise, but if she's already feeling low about her badly paid job she might feel like you're rubbing her nose in it

Sometimes, it can help if you point out your own insecurities, but be warned – this can backfire. She may just use it as fodder for her comments the next time you're out (though if she does, she's no real friend and you should wonder why you're putting up with her).

And if you try all the tips and your mate is still being a nightmare? There's only one solution. Find yourself a real friend who doesn't act like a bitch the whole (or even part) of the time. Life's too short to waste on friends that bring you down.

You Must Be My Best Friend ...

Claire's story: Our friendship stopped swinging

I used to go to swing dancing classes with my friend Becky. We both started at the same time and thought it was fantastic. Not only was it a good way to spend time together and have a good laugh, but we got to meet new people, do a bit of exercise and learn a new skill. I used to come back exhausted, but having thoroughly enjoyed myself.

After a few months, we'd just started getting more confident at it, but Becky got more and more reluctant about going. There was a party bit after the class when anyone could dance with whoever they liked, and for me this was actually the most fun part. Becky had started making a few comments now and then, such as, 'No one wants to dance with me,' and, 'Everyone wants to dance with you,' but I hadn't really realised there was a problem. Her comments had made me feel uncomfortable, but I'd tried to laugh them off and joked that one of the guys was madly in love with *her*. But then she started to get really insecure about her looks, and started making bitchy remarks after the classes. She claimed I was flirting with all the men there and it was 'just' because I was blonde that they wanted to dance with me.

I never really felt Becky was sitting on the sidelines that much, but I guess her insecurities had magnified her feelings when she did have to sit out a dance. In the end she stopped going altogether and I had to give up a really fun hobby – I tried going on my own, but it just wasn't the same without her.

But if it means the little green monster doesn't get in the way of our friendship then it's probably a good thing.

I still see Becky and we have a good laugh, although I'm always a bit worried if someone tries to chat me up when we're together that she'll get annoyed. Until she gets over her issues I think it's always going to be a bit of a problem, but I don't want to lose our friendship because of it. I guess you've just got to take the good and bad of everyone, and she's got enough good qualities for it not to bother me too much.

Ten ways to keep your friendship balanced

1. Don't expect your friend to do all the running; put effort in yourself too.
2. Take it in turns to pick where you go out socially together.
3. Pay your own way – and think about your friend's finances before deciding to book an expensive night out.
4. Take responsibility for your own life, and let your friends take responsibility for theirs …
5. … but don't be afraid to ask for support when you need it, or give support to a friend in crisis.
6. Listen to your friends as much as you talk to them.
7. Confess any jealousies rather than trying to drag your friend down to your perceived level.

You Must Be My Best Friend ...

8. Avoid competing with a friend; her successes don't have any bearing on your failures. You're both individuals.
9. Don't expect to be the best at everything you do — allow your friend her time of glory too.
10. Remember, you aren't the centre of the universe (except on your birthday and wedding day, when it's allowed).

Chapter Four

When Friends Collide

By now, you'd think you'd dealt with most of the issues that could crop up with a mate. But oh no — it gets more complicated, because very few people have only one friend. Indeed, many people have various friendship groups: friends from their childhood, university, the local pub, family friends, work mates — the list goes on.

While your friendship groups *can* be easily integrated, at times it can be tricky. Introducing your best friend from school days — who went tadpoling with you and can remember your first kiss with the school nerd — to your university pal — who knows more about your capacity to down cocktails on a night out and sees you as a bit of a Mata Hari — can be inviting trouble, not to mention embarrassment when they start swapping stories.

*

You Must Be My Best Friend ...

THIRD-WHEEL SYNDROME

Some people believe that all their friends should get on with each other, working on the belief that if Person A likes them, and Person B likes them, then Person A should like Person B. This is flawed logic. After all, people are complicated – the main reason that Person A likes you could be your extensive knowledge of every chick-lit novel ever written, whereas Person B may be attracted to the way that you can keep calm in a crisis. Remember, most people have a number of masks they wear – not just the adult/parent/child masks but also more social ones, like 'Party Girl', 'Man Eater' or 'Career Woman'. Playing different roles with different people is entirely normal (though by far the healthiest way to behave is to just be yourself with everyone), but it can make integrating friendship groups even more complicated.

If you introduce friends to each other and they don't get on, don't panic. It could be that they like different aspects of your personality but don't have anything in common other than a mutual affection for you. It could also be that they feel insecure or threatened by the other person – particularly if one or both of them are people you'd consider to be 'best friends'. They may worry that you like the other person more than you like them, and that they'll get to spend less time with you or feel less affectionate towards them as a result.

And it's not just differences that can make people dislike each other. You may have two friends who you think will get

When Friends Collide

on with each other brilliantly because they're so similar. However, people can sometimes take an instant dislike to someone who's similar to them. For example, let's say you have two loud pals. They won't necessarily recognise this trait in themselves but when confronted with someone else who's loud, will automatically see it as a major issue because they're projecting their own insecurities onto that person. The worst thing that you can say in this situation is 'but you're so similar,' – both people will see it as a slight. Instead, highlight the other attributes that your friends have and show the differences between them.

Another reason that similar people may hate each other is because one or both of them is very competitive. If you have two successful career mates, for example, they may clash because both of them define themselves in that way and they want to prove that they're the better career woman of the two. Whatever you do, never join in with any comparison games – otherwise you could end up losing one or both of them because there's no right thing to say in this situation.

It can seem like a personal insult if your friends don't get on with each other. After all, there is at least a degree of emotional connection between friends and, much as you can say what you want about your own family but if someone else makes a negative comment about them, you'll rise to their defence, the same can be true with friendships.

The best way to deal with friends who don't get on with each other is to make sure that you divide your time fairly between them. If you have limited time and know that you generally have to 'double up' seeing friends in a group rather than on a one-to-one basis, keep your friends feeling connected to you by catching up with them over the phone or email. It's also worth explaining to them that you would love to spend more time with them on their own if you were able to — and apologising — so that they know it's not a personal snub.

If your friends don't get on with each other, it can make social events like birthdays and weddings a nightmare to organise. This is where you have to think laterally. You could just go with the option of telling both your friends that they have to 'play nice' because it's your big day. If, however, there's a major reason why they can't be in the same room without things descending into a row (say, Person A had an affair with Person B's husband and you're unfortunate enough to know and like both of them), then divide your events up. Have a birthday party that starts in a bar and then goes on to your flat afterwards, inviting one friend to one half of the party and another to the other half — telling them in advance that that's what you're doing so that things don't get complicated during 'change-over'. Or invite one friend to the wedding and another to the reception. If you're asked how you decided which one to invite to which event, say that you tossed a coin. That way, your friends are less likely to feel that you chose one of them above the other for the 'better' half of the event (and you can guarantee, whichever half they aren't invited to is the one they'll perceive as 'better' — again, it's just human nature).

When Friends Collide

Sabrina's story: Wedding list hell

I'd always dreamed of getting married so when I met Stewart and we fell in love, I was blissfully happy when he proposed. That was before we had to do the wedding list. He and I have an overlapping social circle but there are a couple of his friends who are nightmares; one of them in particular is a problem. He came on to my best mate one night and wouldn't take no for an answer – she and I both thought that he was an odious creep. Even though he was drunk at the time, it just wasn't acceptable.

Another one of my friends, Mary, had a massive falling out with my friend Petra after Petra accused her of bringing up her daughter to be a hooligan because she's got a liberal approach to child-rearing.

Stewart and I spent hours going through the list, adding people and then removing them because if we invited one person, we'd have to invite another one of their friends who had caused problems with another friend in some way.

In the end, we decided to have three receptions: one the night before the wedding, one on the wedding day and one the day after we got back from honeymoon – and to only invite a few family members and a couple of extremely close friends to the wedding itself. It was the only way that we could possibly have an event that didn't descend into chaos.

I'm glad that I got married – and much as I love Stewart, a big reason for that is that at least I know I'm never going to have to go through creating a wedding invitation list again.

*

You Must Be My Best Friend ...

It's not just friends hating each other that can cause problems. Jealousy can take multiple roles in friendship groups; we all want our friends to get on with each other but if you introduce your two best friends to each other, the last thing you really want deep down is for them to get on better with each other than they do with you. It may not be very mature but, if we're honest, most people feel threatened in that situation.

This is where being in control of your own insecurities is important. Just because your two best friends get on with each other brilliantly, it doesn't mean that they like you any less – there isn't a limited amount of 'like' that someone has, after all. Make sure that you keep the communication flow open, and say if you have an issue with anything as soon as it arises. That way it won't fester and damage the relationship further.

Bear in mind that three can be an awkward number and that it's natural for people in a triumvirate to also split off into pairings at times. If your two best friends go out together without you, it doesn't mean that they're going off you. It's just that sometimes two is an easier number: going out as a threesome can be tricky as one person is always going to be excluded from the conversation, and getting three people to agree on somewhere to go is always harder than if it's just two of you.

Similarly, just because your two best friends get on, don't feel obliged to always invite both of them out at the same time. A one-to-one conversation has a different dynamic than a group conversation, and is an essential part of keeping the intimacy in your friendship.

The point at which friendship threesomes can become a major issue is if two of the three people end up sneaking around behind the other's back to see each other. This can feel hurtful for the excluded party and the dishonesty is unnecessary. If you find that it's going on then it should be confronted – though not in an antagonistic way as there could be an innocent explanation (like your two pals organising a surprise birthday party for you!). Say to your friends that you are really glad that they get on and obviously don't mind them seeing each other on their own, but that you feel excluded and hurt by the deception. It will probably turn out that they genuinely didn't realise that it makes you feel insecure and will both be apologetic.

If they can't see why deception is a problem, and aren't prepared to be honest with you, consider exactly how strong the friendship you have with them really is. However, you should also be aware that it can be a little 'control-freaky' if you insist on knowing every time your pals go out with each other – after all, they don't expect you to call them every time you go out with someone else (do they?).

At root, if you feel bad about something your friends are doing, confront them about it and they aren't prepared to change, be prepared to cut them out of your social circle. Life's too short to waste your time on people who hurt you.

You Must Be My Best Friend ...

Tania's story: They cut me out

I had a best friend, and also a flatmate whom I was close to. I'm not a jealous friend so when they started hanging out together, it wasn't a problem; for me, if people in my life get on together, it's a good thing. When they started telling other friends not to tell me they were hanging out together, THAT was a problem. Eventually, it ended up that the flatmate was going to be a bridesmaid at my best friend's wedding as well as me. No problem for me! It wasn't my wedding and I was honoured to be involved anyway – but they decided not to tell me until after I left the country to go travelling. THAT was a problem.

I was really hurt, but at the same time hugely scathing of both of them: what did they expect me to do – scream and shout? Eventually the bride-to-be decided to tell me about the flatmate being a bridesmaid, although I already knew, and I told her as such.

What the whole situation made clear to me was the level of deception they were prepared to go to with me, supposedly a close friend. It was like having a boyfriend sleeping with your best friend (which has also happened to me), because you still feel stupid, you still feel hurt, you still wonder what you did. Now, I don't talk to either of them. I don't need deceptive people like that in my life and while I hope they're happy, really I don't give a toss. It wasn't easy to become like this and, really, I'd prefer to still have my friends but, at the end of the day, I was

When Friends Collide

shut out of a three-way friendship and it really hurt. It made me feel that, probably, they had never been real friendships anyway. Sadly, it also made me wary about making new friends, and about them getting along with each other. This is a loss for me, but luckily I still have fantastic friends who I know would never do things like that.

And then there's the hellish situation where you introduce two friends and they seem to get on a little bit too well when they discuss the main thing they have in common – you. They might tease you about your silly habits and flaws or tell you *exactly* what they think of your new boyfriend. It's all very well when it's just one friend joking around, but when they join forces it feels like they're ganging up on you and can be a lot more difficult to take. Or, even worse, they might start talking about you behind your back, which is when the ugly subject of gossip can rear its head.

YOU'LL NEVER GUESS WHAT ...

Sharing confidences is one way that people invite intimacy, and it can be all too easy to try to develop a friendship by exchanging gossip. If you're the area of common ground that two friends share, it's all too easy for you to be the person that they talk about. And if you're introducing friends to each other, it can

You Must Be My Best Friend ...

be all too easy to inadvertently give away confidences they've shared with you, in an effort to make your friends seem more interesting. But don't! Private information is something that only the person it's about is at liberty to divulge to someone else. Giving away secrets is a sure-fire way to lose friends, however well-meaning you are when you share it.

Most people have experienced gossip by the time they reach their twenties (at the very latest), be it sharing or being on the receiving end of it. Humans are social animals, so it's only natural — but it's also a very easy way to hurt people you care about. No matter how careful you are — 'don't tell anyone I told you and keep it to yourself but ...' — there's always a risk that the gossip you've shared will get back to the person it's about, with you named as the culprit who leaked it.

Sari's story: I thought that I was safe

I used to 'talk' (sign) about all sorts of personal stuff in public places with a deaf friend of mine, because I was confident that no one around us could understand a word we were signing. This proved to be a big mistake when once on a tube I told him about a friend of mine who had started secretly going out with the father of her (later ex-)boyfriend. How was I supposed to know that the woman sitting opposite us could not only sign, but was actually the (later ex-)wife of the (later ex-)boyfriend's father? Oops!

*

Obviously, the best way to avoid this situation is not to deal in gossip, but it can be tricky when you're chatting to someone and they give you a juicy bit of dirt about another person in your social group, particularly if there's some form of sex or debauchery involved … The natural response to gossip is to trade back something equally salacious. Instead, hold fire. You can invite just as much intimacy by sharing something about yourself. Just make sure that it's not so sordid that you'd feel gutted if you end up hearing it around your friendship-group rumour-mill …

Similarly, to keep yourself in line, if someone tells you something personal, 'return' it with an equally personal bit of info about yourself. Fear is a basic human emotion and your worry about your secret coming out will help you keep your mouth shut about your mate's story.

If you do end up breaching a friend's trust and sharing private information about her, you have two options. Either ignore it, and hope that it will go away – possibly making a call to the person you shared the secret with, reiterating how important it is that they keep it to themselves – or take the mature route, confess and apologise. Your friendship may be tainted for a while afterwards while you rebuild your friend's trust, but at least you know she'll never find out what you did in some other way, which would damage the friendship more terminally.

Don't beat yourself up too much about sharing gossip; if the friend you've talked about is really honest with herself, she'll have to admit that she's shared information that she shouldn't have as well. If, however, you're a serial gossip, you need to take yourself in hand. Either get some counselling to learn how to control it, or find an alternative outlet. This is where friends outside your social circle, and ideally abroad, come in.

There's always a risk that secrets can get passed on if you share them with someone else who lives in the area, even if they don't know the target (or you think that they don't know them). However, if you make a friend over the internet who lives in another country thousands of miles away, the gossip you've shared is much less likely to get back to your mate. Just make damned sure that you never introduce your friend to them over the internet or your entire ruse will backfire horribly. And for God's sake learn how to delete your conversation logs after you've finished your chat. The last thing you want is written proof of exactly what you've said that could, however inadvertently, get found by your friend.

Go on, go on, go on ...

Even if you introduce your friends to each other and they get on well, and you manage to resist the temptation to spread gossip, there's still room left for more conflict in friendship groups, thanks to the wonders of peer pressure. Much as it would be lovely to believe that any mature person will have grown out of taking part in or responding to peer pressure by the time they

When Friends Collide

reach adulthood, sadly it's something that society encourages — think 'keeping up with the Joneses' or following fashion.

Added to this, peer pressure isn't always that obvious. When you're a kid, it's likely that peer pressure will be pretty overt: 'We're all going shoplifting — if you don't come you're not our friend any more,' or, 'You're not painting your bedroom blue are you? We've all got pink bedrooms.' But as you get older, peer pressure is still there — it's just more subtle. For example, you may love Italian food but your two best pals both prefer Japanese so you generally end up go along with them when it comes to picking a restaurant. After all, most people don't want to 'make a fuss' or 'rock the boat'. If your friends are all into clubbing, even though you'd rather spend a night in watching videos and eating pasta with them, chances are you'll end up going along with them and dancing until dawn (even if you are sulking inside). So stop.

Remember, your friends like you for who you are, not for what you do, so don't feel obliged to always go along with what they want. Tell them if you're not in the mood to do something that they suggest, and come up with an alternative. As a kid, it's easy to believe that someone will go off you if you don't do what they say but as an adult, you should be able to trust in your friendships enough that if you have a difference of opinion on what to do, it's no big deal.

Similarly, if you have a strong personality, it can be easy to slip into inadvertently inflicting peer pressure on your friends. Make sure that it's not always you that decides where you go as a group, or what you're doing. If you're the social ringleader, use that responsibility to ensure that everyone gets a fair hearing, in particular people who may feel uncomfortable about speaking out. Friendship is about sharing, and if you can't all share your time together in ways that you all enjoy then you may as well give up on having those friends.

Lucie's story: Friendless and happy

I'm proud to say that I have no friends any more. I moved from Manchester to Suffolk (250 miles) in 2001, much to my friends' disgrace. They thought I should stay so I could carry on hanging out with them/going on family holidays because their husbands didn't want to/fulfilling girly night obligations. I should say that my son was four at the time and some of my friends had children of similar ages. Unlike them I had escaped (literally) a violent and abusive relationship with absolutely nothing to show for it, and was going through a divorce. When the chance came to get away from Manchester I jumped at it. Swap traffic jams/car crimes/violence/sprawling council estates for green/quiet/fluffy bunnies/good schools/villages - it wasn't a difficult choice.

I had a very close relationship with one friend particularly - her eldest son was just a week younger than mine. Holidays/day trips/nights out and in - we were really more like family. This went tits up when I decided to move - she really couldn't understand why I would want to move to a place where I knew no one and

When Friends Collide

had no job. Every time I phoned her she would ask when I was coming back. I wanted her to be pleased for me - I had managed to find a good job really quickly, lived in a lovely village, had met a new man (who I now live with) - why would I give it up? So I just don't bother to call her any more, and she doesn't call me either. It doesn't actually worry me at all.

Funnily enough my partner is exactly the same. Neither of us can be bothered with the pressures friends will put on you to do as they wish. I have work colleagues, which also involves the occasional function, and other mums that I know through my son's after-school club - they organise various social events to raise funds, and I'm more than happy to attend an adult disco in the village hall. These people fulfil any social requirements, combined with our love of eating out and days at the beach, without me feeling the need to spend hours on the phone chatting to them or have them drink wine in my lounge.

Having said that I am considering starting a book club - but this is probably more to fulfil my love of reading and share it with like-minded people. At least I can structure this, in that they will appear in my lounge, or me in theirs, on a certain day at a certain time and they will piss off after a few hours and leave me to sit on my sofa in my dressing gown watching TV.

People like Lucie are very rare though. Most of us need more than just our partner to keep us entertained. After all, if your

You Must Be My Best Friend ...

partner is your only friend and anything goes wrong with the relationship, you're left alone — something that most of us are scared of. Though, on the plus side, with only one friend at least there's no likelihood of them clashing with other pals.

TEN WAYS TO STOP FRIENDS COLLIDING

1. Don't expect your friends to all get on with each other. Even if they're similar to each other, they may well be jealous (even subconsciously) of you having a close relationship with someone else.
2. Divide your time fairly between your friends; that doesn't mean equally, but according to how much you like them.
3. If you're jealous of the way that your two best friends get on with each other, tell them: they both care about you so will be mindful of your feelings.
4. Remember, there isn't a limited amount of 'like' that anyone has so if your friends get on well with each other, it doesn't mean they like you any less.
5. Don't bow to peer pressure, or inflict it on anyone else.
6. If someone repeatedly hurts you, through gossip or any other means, cut them out of your life.
7. Avoid gossiping about your friends. If you must share gossip, make friends who are at least a continent away, over the internet, and gossip with them instead.

When Friends Collide

8. If you're a serial gossip, train yourself out of it by always exchanging a piece of gossip about yourself when someone shares a secret with you. The fear of them breaching your confidence will help train you out of it.
9. If you meet another pal of your best friend's, don't gang up on your best friend; even light-hearted comments can be hurtful.
10. Avoid three-way friendships if at all possible: they're horribly complicated.

Chapter Five

Sex and Friendship

Whether you're gay, straight or bi, at some stage, sex will enter into your friendship. You might not actually get down and dirty but if you get to 30 and have never had an undercurrent of sexual tension with a friend, sorry, but it just means that you never noticed they were secretly pining for you. And changes in society have increased the chance that sex will enter (quite literally) into the friendship equation. Sexuality is now accepted as being more ambiguous (or at least, there's less stigma attached to being gay, lesbian or bi than there once was, in part thanks to more media representations: from the lesbian fling in *Sex and the City* to *Queer as Folk* and *The L Word*). As a result, your friendship group is more likely to contain someone who's at least openly bisexual than it would have done ten years ago.

Similarly, once upon a time, men and women couldn't be friends. It was thought to be unseemly – after all, if a man and woman spent time together, surely there had to be something more than just friendship going on, didn't there? Then came feminism, and general developments in society, and all of a sudden the male–female friendship was born. But there's still an aura of sex hanging over those friendships, as the film *When Harry Met Sally* so ably demonstrates.

As we all know, the second that sex gets involved, life gets much more complicated. One person's meaningless fling can be another's ultimate fantasy that they've been pining about for years. Even worse, one person's drunken attempt at a kiss can be another person's utter betrayal of the friendship. Regardless of the way either or both of you feel about what happens, it's a rare friendship that can continue completely unchanged once sex enters the equation.

Sara's story: Why *When Harry Met Sally* is mostly evil

I think that every woman has seen the movie *When Harry Met Sally* and it leads to the kind of heartache only dreamed about by poets. Now, this is what I know as a slightly disillusioned, single 28-year-old: Boys and girls are different in that boys know in the first 15 nanoseconds whether or not they would go out with a girl (based on her looks) and girls take time to warm up as they understand that there is more to someone than the way their upper parts jiggle in a Juicy sweatshirt. I'm not saying that a dude will pledge his life to a woman in the first 15 seconds, but he relegates her into one of three categories: 1) I would date

Sex and Friendship

her, 2) I would sleep with her or 3) his mother. Category number two is where most women end up, which is fine, but they are slotted there in the first glances. Once in category number two, there is no going back to category number one: you are in 'sleep with her limbo'.

Now if a girl makes friends with a guy and she grows to like him and he has relegated her to category number two, he will in fact get drunk and sleep with her all the while telling her perfectly lovely things because he is in euphoria over actually succeeding in taking her pants off. This is even the case when the two of them are very good friends because in his heart every dude knows that girl nakedness is limited, so they are not going to look a gift boob in the mouth.

The situation changes if the girl was previously attached and the man has been pining away for her, but the theory still applies because she was always in category number one.

Now, that was all explanation for this: *When Harry Met Sally* is in fact impossible because no dude will ever move his friend, who is a girl from category number two, to category number one after ten years. The sleeping together part is the most realistic part of the whole movie; the romantic comedy, made-up part is his desire to marry her. What should have happened is that they slept together, he bolted, freaked out, called the next day and blathered on about how she is amazing, but that their friendship means to much to him for it to go any further, then pretended it never happened. She, however, would be left in a tangle of girl guilt and confusion because he said lovely things about her and then they did it, which in some worlds is an indicator of interest in dating – but not in boy world.

Then she would analyse everything that happened with all of her girlfriends incessantly for two weeks. The two people would drift apart as friends because the girl already has a huge collection of people and doesn't need him, he was just around because she wanted to date him; and he won't want her to get the wrong idea. So you see, that is why I think that *When Harry Met Sally* is Slightly Evil – because it is a cute movie, but total fantasy.

THE FRIENDSHIP/SEX RULES

By far the easiest solution is to keep sex entirely separate from friendship – but then, that's up there in 'ideal world' territory alongside never having to pay any taxes and waking up with perfect hair every single morning, regardless of how heavy a session you had the night before. Like it or not, we live in an increasingly sexualised society. And with the rise in bicuriosity, even same-sex friendships can have a sexual charge to them. So what to do?

To start with, it's worth making sure that you're on the 'same page' as your friends sex-wise. If your pal fancies you, it's much better to know, as that way you won't inadvertently lead them on by flirting (well, not if you're a nice person who genuinely sees them as a friend). If you discover that your friend is into you and you don't feel the same way, certain things should be taken as read – for example, you should never share a bed with a friend who has a crush on you if you don't fancy them back. It's the worst possible tease behaviour and really not fair towards someone you like. However, don't avoid talking about other people you fancy in front of them – you need to make sure that your friend knows that they don't have a chance with you as, that way, they can hopefully move on and find someone who *is* into them.

Similarly, if you have a crush on a friend, it's worth testing the waters with them; the old 'parallel dimension' ruse is a good one. Say something like, 'I've sometimes wondered what would have happened if we'd met each other differently and had ended up dating instead of being friends.' This couches your confession in a fictitious scenario, which makes it a lot easier for your friend to be honest with you. If he says, 'Yeah, I've thought the same thing,' then you could be on to a winner and may find that things can start getting more heated. If, however, they say, 'God, could you imagine – what a nightmare,' then you know that the feeling is in no way reciprocated and can make a joke out of it.

I love you, you're my best mate ...

Of course, you're then into the problem of what to do if you fancy a friend and they don't fancy you back. This really depends on your own personality. If you're the kind of person who can go, 'Oh well,' and move on to your next target then fair enough. But if it's going to feel like a knife through your heart every time that your friend talks about someone they fancy/introduces you to a partner/leches after a film star when you go to the movies together, then, sorry, the best thing that you can do for your emotional health is to let that friendship go. Explain the situation to your friend — over the phone or email if it's too hard or embarrassing for you to do face-to-face — so that they don't try to contact you and make it harder for you to maintain your resolve. It may hurt like hell at the time but you're saving yourself potential years of heartbreak. Added to this, if you're hanging out with someone you're secretly in love with, it will send off 'I'm not available for a relationship' vibes to any other tasty totty, blowing your chances of finding anyone else.

GIRLS WHO LOVE GIRLS, AND BOYS WHO LOVE BOYS

With around ten per cent of people being lesbian or gay and many more bicurious (particularly women), it's not that uncommon for sex to enter the equation in same-gender friendships. If both of you are lesbian or gay, you may be able to talk about it openly, following the guidelines above. But if you're broadly straight and have a crush on a same-sex friend, things can be more complicated. First off, don't automatically assume that it makes you a lesbian/gay. Over a third of women fantasise about sex with another woman, and 15 per cent of men fantasise about other blokes.

Sex and Friendship

If you're friends with someone foxy then it's not remotely uncommon for your fantasies to revolve around them. It's easy for human emotions to get mixed up, and if your friend is being supportive, kind and thoughtful, it can be easy to confuse platonic love with erotic love. The absolute worst thing that you can do in this situation is to get drunk and make a lunge.

Instead, if you're female, talk about it with her — women are generally much better at having emotional conversations than men so it should be relatively easy to bring up the subject. Keep the conversation light — maybe mention the whole topic of bicuriosity to her (say you've read an article about it recently if you'd feel uncomfortable bringing it up apropos of nothing) and see what her response is like. If she says, 'That's gross,' or similar then you'll know it's definitely safest to keep your crush to yourself (in which case, you should also look at whether you're able to maintain the friendship with her or if it will be too emotionally tricky for you). If, however, she is enthusiastic about the idea, ask about her ideal woman. Chances are, she'll ask you who your ideal woman is afterwards, giving you the opportunity to jokingly say, 'Well, you and I are best friends and you're a bit of a babe, so someone like you would be pretty cool.' Again, keep it light so that if she recoils in horror you can say, 'Yeah, well, obviously not you because I know you too well and you're my pal — I meant someone like you. Duh!'

If you're male, it can be trickier as homophobia is more rife in men (possibly because there's less boy/boy imagery in the

You Must Be My Best Friend ...

media, so we're not programmed to find it as visually appealing). However, you can use a similar tack — subtle references that lead into a conversation. Sound out your pal's attitudes by talking about a gay friend (he can be fictitious). If this leads to a lot of scorn and jibes about 'poofters' or 'fudge-packers' your friend probably won't be up for a stubbly snog (even if it's only because he has a knee-jerk reaction down to secret desires). If he suggests the pair of you go to a club with your mate, then who knows, your luck could be in.

Be aware that if things do progress sexually with a same-sex friend and it's the first time for either or both of you, your friendship may be strained by any sexual encounter. Some people who have a same-sex experience feel immensely guilty afterwards and/or go into crisis mode, thinking that they must be a lesbian/gay and are going to have to change their life. As a result, your friend may decide to cut you out of their life for making them confront a side of themselves that they're not happy with. Then again, they may decide that they're madly in love and you two are perfect for each other. Or you could have any of those reactions yourself. If you're lucky, you'll both feel the same way afterwards but it's impossible to know what someone's response will be until it happens, so be incredibly careful and make sure that you both know exactly what you want before things get heated. It won't guarantee that things don't get complicated but it will give you a greater chance of maintaining the friendship regardless of what happens between you.

Sex and Friendship

Ros' story: We experimented together

Lucia and I met through a mutual ex-boyfriend. From the moment we met, we got on brilliantly - even better than either of us did with him. The night that he introduced us to each other, we ended up chatting solidly all night and pretty much ignoring him. It seemed like she was my clone - we'd studied the same thing at university, had a similar relationship history and even used the same slang words as each other. We arranged to meet up the following weekend without our ex, so that we could carry on getting to know each other.

We soon become good friends: we were on the phone most days and the conversations always lasted for hours. We got into a habit of staying at each other's houses whenever we went out to save cab fare - and so that we could carry on talking until the early hours. A lot of the time, our conversation focused around sex: both of us are highly sexed and were going through a stage of working our way through half the city's male population.

One night, after a lot of drink, Lucia asked me if I'd ever thought about being with a woman. I admitted that I'd fantasised about it, ever since a girl had kissed me in a club years back, but I'd never done anything about it. She asked me if I found her attractive and I said I did. The next thing I knew, we were kissing. It was wonderful - much softer and more sensual than being with a man. One thing led to another and we ended up in bed together, trying everything we'd ever thought about.

The next morning, it was a bit embarrassing. I wasn't sure if she wanted things to go further – I was fine spending a night with her but I didn't want a girlfriend. Luckily, we decided to talk about it and agreed that it was a one-off that had been fun but nothing else. We even ended up telling our ex about it. Obviously, he wanted all the gory details, being a man, but we kept them to ourselves. It's much funnier watching him squirm and imagine all the things that we might have got up to. Despite much pleading from him – he wants to watch us – we've never repeated the experience.

KEEPING IT PLATONIC

Despite the many issues that can be raised (ahem), there are many, many successful male–female friendships out there, and sex really doesn't need to cause problems. Even if you do 'slip' and cop off with a friend one night, it can be handled easily enough as long as you talk about it afterwards and are in agreement that it was a one-off and won't happen again (or indeed, are in agreement of any kind). Sure, the next time you're drunk with that mate, you may both get embarrassed that it could happen again – or want to do it again! But it's nothing that can't be easily dealt with by applying self-control and reminding yourself – and each other – that the friendship is the most important thing to you.

Sex and Friendship

Ashley's story: Men and women can be friends

My best friend and I met in junior high (middle school or whatever, we were 12 years old); we were both in the school band. He was the lead trumpet player and I had a huge crush on him, but he was too busy dating everyone else in the band (for a week here and there ... you know how junior high romances go) to date me. Finally, a whole year later, when his best friend was dating my best friend, he asked me out. That lasted for about two weeks, then he dumped me (we never even kissed or anything, so I don't know if you can really consider it a relationship, but whatever).

We went to high school together the next year, and played in the marching band, wind symphony, symphonic band, and jazz band together (any chance I could get to watch him play). He dated people, I dated people, and we remained friendly. Then, one day, he confessed that the only reason he had dated me in junior high was because my best friend felt sorry for me because I had such a big crush on him, and she talked to her boyfriend (his best friend), who in turn offered him money to date me for a couple of weeks. Talk about being absolutely crushed. It makes you feel really good to know that someone only considered dating you because there was cash involved. I was fuming mad, but it had been three years earlier and we had both grown up a lot since then, so I put on that fake smile and pretended not to care. It didn't surprise me, I was the shy awkward kid with frizzy hair, it's not like the boys were lining up for me.

You Must Be My Best Friend ...

We remained friends. I had to respect him for telling me – he didn't have to and I probably never would have found out. The next academic year rolled around and he came back looking better than ever – actually both of us did, that summer was good to us – and we were talking and hanging out more and more, really getting to know one another. One day after school, he finally kissed me. I'd only been waiting five years! We dated for a little over a year, which is a pretty long time for a school relationship and were both pretty happy. I had thinned out a little and learned how to straighten and control my hair, but I was still the shy frizzy girl to everyone at high school. It's amazing how that image can follow you around until you get away from everyone who knew you then – and that's exactly what happened.

He and I played in a drum and bugle corps outside school and I found myself surrounded by a new group of people who never knew me as shy, awkward, or frizzy. All of a sudden (not to sound conceited or anything) a bunch of guys were talking about how 'hot' I was and how they wanted to date me. All that attention can really go to your head and I started hanging out more and more with some of the other guys in the group and paying less and less attention to my boyfriend. I had the attitude, 'Oh well, if he dumps me, one of these other guys will want me.' And eventually he did just that and I hooked up with another guy the next day (against my better judgment). I've never seen anyone so angry or hurt in my entire life. When I realized how much he really did care for me it was my turn to feel upset.

Sex and Friendship

We didn't talk for a couple of months, although we saw each other everyday because we were playing in a bunch of groups together. After we'd both cooled down I realized how much I missed his friendship and I started trying to talk to him more and more, and he came around after a while. We were able to put our past behind us and he's literally my best friend now. He knows me better than anyone; he knows first hand how I was in junior high, high school, outside school, has seen me change and mature, and I've seen the same in him.

Since high school we've gone our separate ways. He moved about 20 minutes away, but we still talk on the phone and see each other whenever possible. We discuss absolutely everything from day to day activities to our current relationships. I've run all of my new boyfriends by him and I take his opinion seriously (as much as I hate to admit it, he's usually right; he can predict my actions/feelings with amazing accuracy). I listen to his relationship woes and give my advice. We've even gone out on double dates.

I love him to death, but I'm not in love with him, and there is a big difference in my book. We're definitely not right for each other for the long haul, and we both know that. He drives me absolutely mad if I have to put up with him for more than a few hours at a time (I'm sure the feeling is mutual), but we need each other for support and advice here and there, and we have the unique kind of relationship where we can be brutally (and I mean BRUTALLY) honest with one another and know that our friendship will survive.

You Must Be My Best Friend ...

And so, in response to the age-old question, 'Can men and women truly be friends?' ... Yes. I feel that my friend and I are a perfect example of a purely platonic relationship between two people of the opposite sex.

Staying friends with the ex

Sex doesn't always enter the equation *after* you become friends. Sometimes it can precede it – when you turn an ex-partner into a friend. Of all the kinds of friendship, staying pals with your ex can be the trickiest, particularly if you've been in a long-term relationship together. Some people try to cling on to a previous relationship by using the 'let's be friends' line. If that's the case then it's not going to be a healthy friendship – one (or both) of you will be constantly trying to either win the other one back or prove that you're 'so over' your ex. Alternatively, you'll both end up using the friendship as a pseudo-relationship – and probably keep falling into the sack with each other every time that you've had one too many. Not only is this damaging to your self-esteem – you can start seeing yourself good enough to be a friend but not good enough to have a relationship – but it will also stop you from moving on and finding someone who is right for you.

Sex and Friendship

Gavin's story: Sex messed things up

I had a very close female friend. She was not only my friend; in the medieval group that I belong to she was my consort; when I fought, I fought for her honour. You can't really remain that close without something happening so eventually we started sleeping together, which in turn became dating.

Things weren't always wonderful; we had a few ups and downs as couples do, but we worked pretty well together, I thought. Until she decided that we needed a break. Of course when she said 'we' what she meant was 'I' and when she said 'need a break' what she meant was 'want to break up with you'.

As you can guess I was somewhat unhappy with this arrangement as I loved her, but what can you do? It takes two committed people to maintain a relationship so I said fair enough and we remained friends. Actually we still remained good friends, we still hung out a lot, still crashed in each other's bed and even tried the 'no strings attached' sex thing.

Well, after three months she decided that she was going to go back and date her ex-boyfriend again. Again I was unhappy, because I was hoping that we would get back together ... you can't not really, can you? OK, so she was back with her ex-boyfriend and we still remained friends, because that's what friends do, isn't it? They stick by each other no matter what? At least that's what I thought.

OK, so what we have here is a girl who has dated me, dumped me, got back with her ex and throughout all this I

You Must Be My Best Friend ...

remained her friend and stuck by her through all the problems she's had. And all this is going along quite well, until of course I began seeing someone. (OK, so it was her cousin, but still, she'd dumped me over three months prior and had got back with her ex-boyfriend.)

Now, apparently, I am the bane of her existence and the cause of all that is evil and debased in the world. She won't go to a party if she thinks I might be there, and if we do happen to be at the same event she ignores me as if I'm someone that she has never laid eyes on before; no, worse that that, if I was a stranger she might at least be wondering who I was.

Things haven't got any better. I wonder how she's going to react when she finds out I'm marrying her cousin? What a waste of a good friendship.

However, if you've had a relationship with someone and it works on every level except sexually then maintaining a friendship can be a good thing. If you've spent time getting to know someone and have a lot in common with them, why throw the baby out with the bathwater and refuse to see them altogether just because you're no longer getting physical with each other?

If you are going to be friends with an ex, it's worth bearing in mind a few basic rules. To start with, always allow the dust to settle — don't see each other the day after you've split up because you'll just end up re-hashing all the reasons that you broke up

Sex and Friendship

in the first place. Try to give it at least a fortnight – longer if it was a serious relationship and/or one or both of you was in love – because otherwise you're likely to get stuck in a loop of rows and recriminations (or at the very least, falling into bed with each other).

You should also have a discussion with your ex about the way that you'll handle each other dating again. Some people find it easiest to go straight in and hear all the gory details because that way they can get over the pain quicker, and move you mentally into the 'friend' category far more quickly. Others find that they're happy with the idea of their ex dating someone else but don't feel ready to hear anything other than a brief 'I've got a date on Saturday' in the early stages of the friendship. If you bring up the subject of dating with your ex and they refuse to talk about it at all, examine the friendship; they're probably not over you yet and, as such, it's not that good an idea to stay friends – at least until the pain has gone away.

Candy's story: I convert them into friends

I'm friends with almost all of my exes. Just because someone isn't romantically right for me, I don't see why that means all the rest of the stuff has to get thrown out. When I was younger, I thought that I was being emotionally mature by doing this - 'see how relaxed I am, I can get over an ex and

You Must Be My Best Friend ...

stay friends with them,' – but as I've got older, I'm less sure. I'm beginning to think that I might keep them as friends because I can't let go – part of me secretly wants them to realise what a mistake they made and come running back to me.

It's not that I'd even want to be with most of them any more – getting to know them as friends means that I know more of their bad habits, apart from anything else. But I've noticed that I'm a lot closer to them whenever I'm single and they are too. I'm much more flirtatious if I think I've got a chance of winning them back – or at least making them want me, if only for the night.

Staying friends with exes has led to some embarrassing situations too – where I've had a party and realised that two of my exes are chatting to each other. I'm always paranoid that they're talking about me when that kind of thing happens, which isn't good for my self-esteem. And it puts me off pulling anyone else in front of them too.

I'm not sure whether I'll bother trying to stay friends with any future exes. It feels like you've got a constant reminder of being single: you're not good enough to go out with half of your friends. I just don't think it's good for your sense of security.

Overall, when it comes to friendships with exes, handle with care. A friendship may seem like a relationship minus the sex, but it's a lot harder to deal with the reduction in intimacy if you've previously allowed someone into your heart.

Sex and Friendship

WHEN PARTNERS GET JEALOUS

Even if you don't have any sexual feelings towards your friends and they aren't attracted to you, sex can still be an issue, courtesy of whoever both of you are dating. This is particularly common in straight friendships: the whole male–female friendship concept is still new enough to leave room for insecurity. (That said, if you're gay and hanging round with hot totty every night, chances are your lover won't appreciate it much either.)

The love of your life may well feel incredibly threatened by the fact that there's another person who you share your innermost thoughts with. They might also think that there must be something sexual going on because they're convinced that everyone would fancy you as much as they do and/or no one could ever be friends with you without wanting sex. All you can do in this scenario is reassure your partner that they're the one for you, and your friends are just that.

If a partner is still insecure, introduce them to your friends to prove that there's nothing going on. And if, after that, your partner still says that he wants you to drop your friends, think about whether they're really someone you want to spend your time with; someone who's that insecure will probably spend his time trying to bring you down too.

Ultimately, the only person who should choose your friends is you. Anyone who tries to convince you otherwise is way too controlling to be able to form a healthy relationship.

You Must Be My Best Friend ...

Pippa's story: Jealousy is a nightmare

I've got as many male friends as female friends. Whenever we go out, I've got a habit of staying over with my mates, as I live in a city and don't have a lot of cash for cabs late at night. As most of my mates are similarly poor, they tend to live in flat-shares, so it's not uncommon for me to end up sharing a bed with a friend – the male ones as well as the female ones. I always wear a T-shirt and knickers, and it's not a sexual thing. It's just down to convenience.

This is all very well when I'm single, but whenever I'm attached, my boyfriends see it as a sign that I'm cheating on them. They don't understand that it's perfectly innocent. I think this is stupid – it shows they're far too possessive for me. But I've got to admit, it's becoming enough of a problem in my relationships now that I'm starting to reconsider. I just wish that men would realise that it's perfectly possible for a woman to have a male friend that she doesn't want to sleep with, even if they do share a bed.

If it's your friend who has a jealous partner, try to be the mature one. Remember, many people are insecure and worry that their partner having a good relationship with another person could have a negative impact on their romantic relationship. It's human nature to feel threatened by someone else who is close to the person that you love. Women are often uncomfortable about their boyfriend having a close girlie pal, particularly if

Sex and Friendship

there's ever been any romance (or even a drunken encounter) between you and their boyfriend. These feelings can manifest themselves in many ways: from being bitchy to the person they feel threatened by to sulking or even getting depressed whenever their partner sees them.

As a good friend, your role is to try to make your friend's partner feel as comfortable as possible about you being around. That said, it's not entirely your responsibility. In a healthy relationship, your friend should be the one making his partner feel secure — and beyond that, she should be getting her confidence from within. But hell, friends help each other out, so play nice.

Laura's story: She couldn't get over our past

A few months after college, my close friend Barry came to my birthday celebration at a local NYC bar and brought his friend Alec along. Alec and I got on well, and over the next few weeks we had a number of dates. However, it quickly became clear to me that this was not the beginning of a great romance, but rather a solid and wonderful friendship with some sex thrown in for fun. While I adored Alec, I didn't feel the sexual or emotional chemistry necessary for exclusivity. And although Alec didn't readily admit it, his heart was still broken from his ex-girlfriend Deepa, who had recently dumped him for a new man. Alec was clearly still pining for her, and was untroubled

You Must Be My Best Friend ...

that I wanted to date other men. In fact, for one blind date I reluctantly agreed to attend, Alec even helped me choose my outfit.

When that dreaded blind date turned out to be a raving success, leading to subsequent dates and the flutter in my stomach that was always missing with Alec, I ended the sexual aspect of my relationship with Alec altogether. Our friendship, however, continued seamlessly. In fact, I think it even got stronger once the sexual pressures and expectations were lifted. Our flirting ended overnight, and neither of us even noticed it was missing. We were just the best of friends, with no sexual tension to speak of.

My relationship with Jason (the blind-date man) turned into love, and for the next three whole years my friendship with Alec stayed strong. Our sexual past was entirely forgotten. So when Deepa broke up with her boyfriend, and she and Alec started seeing each other again, I was thrilled for Alec.

When I finally met her, Deepa and I had an instant connection. I could see immediately why he had loved her all those years, and within only a few weeks, she and I had become friends too.

Deepa and I continued to spend time together and talk, and one day she admitted that she was jealous that Alec and I had once dated. I made it clear to her that our dating had hardly counted for anything, that it was years ago, and that it had ended because he was still in love with her and because I had met Jason, my current boyfriend. She had NOTHING to worry about and no reason to be jealous or threatened.

Sex and Friendship

A few days later, Alec and Deepa were having dinner with some friends, and I was going to meet up with them at a bar afterwards. When I arrived at the bar they weren't there yet so I called Alec's cell phone. He told me they had got held up at the restaurant and would be there in about a half-hour. I was annoyed, so he apologised and offered to pick me up a pastry at the bakery next to the restaurant.

An hour later, they still had not arrived, and it was only after the bar had closed that Alec and Deepa arrived with their friend Paul. It was clear that Alec and Deepa had been fighting, and Paul filled me in on what had happened. Alec had asked Deepa if she'd like anything from the bakery, and she'd said yes. When he returned with two pastries she was furious, realising that he had only gone into the bakery to get me something in the first place. From there it just deteriorated, with Alec yelling at her that SHE had broken up with HIM for another guy all those years ago, and that she had no right to be jealous of his relationship with me. 'What was I supposed to do, never date another woman? Yes, I FUCKED Laura, I FUCKED her for months, and you have to deal with that because YOU broke up with ME for Josh!'

I was livid. I could have killed Alec for making our already difficult situation all but impossible. By taunting his already-jealous girlfriend with our sexual past, I feared that he had put the future of our friendship in serious jeopardy.

The next morning, Alec called her and apologised, and they made up. The damage, however, had been done for Alec and I.

You Must Be My Best Friend ...

After that day, he simply stopped returning my phone calls and disappeared from my life for ever, without so much as a goodbye. I saw that Alec truly loved Deepa and didn't want to risk losing her again. What angered me beyond all possible description, however, and what made me lose all respect for my old friend Alec, was the spineless way he handled the whole issue. For as long as I had known him, Alec had preached continually about the need to 'do the right thing,' to always handle difficult situations with dignity and to treat people with respect. So where was that now?

Ironically, Deepa had the nerve to still want me as her friend. Needless to say, I was no longer interested in the friendship. I lost touch with them both, and I haven't spoken to either of them for two years. The lack of closure on my friendship with Alec bothered me for a while afterwards. However, I came to understand that both Alec and Deepa were afflicted with deep, long-standing insecurities that they simply could not conquer. Their fear of losing each other was overwhelming, and it eclipsed their ability to see the surrounding situation clearly.

The best way to deal with a jealous partner is to meet them and show that they have nothing to fear from you, or feel worried about. (This is not the time to wear your slinkiest frock, or sexiest jeans, OK? The aim here is to look non-threatening.) If you befriend the partner as well then they're less likely to feel concerned if you do spend time with their partner on your own. It doesn't always work – some people are just too insecure to share their partner with anyone else – but it's a good place to start.

Beth's story: She gets in the way

When I split up with my ex, it was all very amicable and we used to see each other most weeks. Then he met Annabel, and they started going out. She hated him seeing me and made it tricky for us to meet up, even though there was nothing going on between us. In the end, she decided – and he agreed – that he could only see me if she came too.

Now, whenever we meet up, it's really strained. I've tried to get on with her but she's very clearly watching the clock and wanting to get things over with as quickly as possible. I can't talk to him about our mutual friends or what's going on in my life without having to give her the background too, which I don't want to do. It's getting to the stage where I don't enjoy meeting up with him any more, because it entails seeing her too and she's such hard work. Unless they split up, I can't see us staying friends for much longer, which makes me feel sad.

It's not just opposite-sex friendships that can be affected by a partner's jealousy; people can get jealous over friends of the same sex, even if not in a sexual jealousy way, particularly if they feel like they don't get to see their partner enough because they're spending all their time with friends.

Too much love can kill you

Sadly, no matter how hard you try, some people are unable to deal with the pressure of getting a hard time from their partner every time they see a friend. As a result, you may find that you get 'dumped' by your friend so that they get an easy life from their other half. Although it can be hurtful if a friend drops you because their partner doesn't like you, try not to get too upset about it. When it comes down to it, most people will put the person they love ahead of friends. Everyone is scared about being alone on some level, and having a partner to share your life with is something that helps alleviate that fear. With any luck, it will be short-lived — someone who wants to control who their partner spends time with will probably be controlling in other ways that can be damaging to a relationship — but if not, accept it and move on.

It's worth bearing in mind that you can pass some of the blame onto science. The chemicals that go through someone's body when they first meet someone they're attracted to are powerful intoxicants. There's oxytocin, endorphins and DHEA which, when added together, are a chemical combination that's remarkably similar to taking an ecstasy tablet. Because of this, even if your friend doesn't drop you entirely, you also shouldn't

Sex and Friendship

be too surprised if they go briefly AWOL when they first meet a new partner. While this can be frustrating – particularly if your friend stands you up repeatedly because their partner takes precedence – it's also very common.

The good news is that most of these chemicals start to fade after about three months, so you can rest assured that it's more than likely that your friend will return to you, probably grovelling and apologising that they ignored you for so long. As a general guide, if you apply the 'three-month rule' – a friend is allowed three months to behave in a loved-up and selfish fashion – then you should be able to avoid getting too hurt and losing a friendship.

However, some people – women in particular – make a habit of this kind of bad behaviour. If you have a friend who constantly 'falls in love' for three months and ignores you, then splits up with her partner and expects the friendship to continue as it did before, then you need to talk to her about it. Point out that you're unhappy with being a friend only when she's single; it may be that she doesn't realise what she's doing. And make your own friendship guidelines. For example, if you make an arrangement to see a friend, that she then wants to cancel, she needs to give you a reasonable amount of notice unless it's something unavoidable (illness/major family issues – not just her boyfriend getting tickets to the cinema). If a friend isn't *ever* prepared to put you first then you may want to think about whether she's someone you really need in your life.

Possessive friends

On the other hand, it might not be the partner that's getting jealous. An alarming amount of people get possessive over their friends and have a hard time adjusting to them getting a new partner. But remember, just because a boy pal enjoys your company as a friend, it doesn't mean that he needs no other women in his life. After all, you're not going to put out (unless you're fuck-buddies, and that's an entirely separate type of friendship) and the poor bloke needs to get his oats somewhere.

SEXUAL JEALOUSY

You'd think after all that lot that every aspect of sex and friendship would be covered. But it's not just fancying a friend, or having some form of conflict with friends because of a relationship that can cause problems. Being single can also bring sexual issues: one friend could find it easy to pull while the other finds it a nightmare and ends up feeling rejected, so taking out those feeling on their 'more attractive' friend. Or you could both fancy the same bloke when you're at a party and end up getting competitive with each other.

Friendship *should* be more important than pulling but, in reality, this often isn't the case. Instead, you need to come up with coping mechanisms: you could agree to take it in turns to get 'first dibs' on an attractive man; decide that neither of you

Sex and Friendship

will go after someone that both of you fancy; or even agree 'best woman wins' and both go for it. Whatever you decide, you should make sure that you both stick to it though — otherwise you're betraying a friend and it's entirely understandable if she doesn't forgive you.

Odette's story: She turned into a bitch

It is amazing how a change in a friend's status can change them from a best friend into a hated bitch. The most recent incident I recall is my now ex sister-in-law. When I was married to her brother, she and I used to hang out and do a lot of fun things together. We truly enjoyed every moment we were together. She would call me all hours of the day or night to get together and I would do likewise. There were no boundaries because we were family.

Before I carry on, I need to mention the following: She is a stereotypical blonde: Beautiful, voluptuous, etc, but as thick as three bricks. She has a heart of gold when you're her friend, but can also be a heinous bitch at the drop of a hat.

So anyway: I was her best friend for the longest time. We turned a lot of heads together because I'm not too shabby looking even if I say so myself, but I'm more the thin, intellectual, small-breasted brunette with an arse that just won't quit type. So together we pretty much covered the taste of most men (and some women, to be totally honest).

You Must Be My Best Friend ...

As I mentioned before we had a lot of good times together while I was happily married to her brother. But then he cheated on me and things began to turn sour. To cut a long story short: I eventually met someone else and introduced my new flame to my then 'best friend'. That was when I began to see her in a different light. She was no longer just the blonde bombshell with whom I could hang out willy-nilly – she and I were now in competitive territory. She is a natural flirt and her little habits of touching men playfully and laughing at every stupid thing they say suddenly became thorns in my side. I no longer saw her as harmless and fun, but as an actual threat to my new relationship. That was when I realised that even though I can hang out with her in public or in crowds and have a good time, I only trust her as far as I can throw her stupid Mini Cooper.

Later, when she eventually got married, her husband, who I became friends with in a totally harmless way, warned me that he could not be in a room alone with me. The reason was not that he had a crush on me or anything like that. It was because his wife hinted that she didn't trust me with him. So I guess it cuts both ways ... 'You must be my best friend because I hate you'.

Or, even worse, if you're single and your friend's attached, you may find yourself fancying her partner. It should go without saying that dating a friend's partner is the lowest of the low thing to do and any good friend won't do it. However, sometimes it happens. If it does, the only reasonable thing to do is tell your friend, apologise gratuitously — and not be surprised if they never want to see you again and bitch about you to all your mutual friends.

Tim's story: He stole my girlfriend

This (ex-)mate of mine (I've known him since first day of high school 1990) broke up with his girlfriend of eight or nine years. He didn't take it too well and stopped going out with our group of friends and generally acting like he was down. So I encouraged him to come out with me and my girlfriend of seven years. He slept at our place some weekends and was generally hanging around a lot of the time.

Now coinciding with this, my relationship with my girlfriend started to deteriorate. We fought regularly (about nothing) and I could see them getting closer and closer to each other, while getting further and further away from me. He was acting weird all the time, and when I talked to him about it he gave the 'I don't want to get involved' excuse. When I talked to her about it and even suggested that it looked like she was more into him than me, she dismissed it.

We broke up (for no apparent reason except that things weren't working out) and in the two weeks following I didn't even get a call from him to talk about it. I finally tracked him down at the pub and talked to him. When I gave him shit for

You Must Be My Best Friend ...

not calling or anything he acted all strange and said, 'I don't want to get involved.' A few drinks later I was still giving him shit for being a bad mate when he came out with, 'I'm in love with her ...' I stared at him, and everything started to make sense.

I kicked my ex-girlfriend out of my place (no idea why she was still living there anyway) and when I confronted her, wanting to know how long it had been happening, her only reply was, 'What do you want me to say?' I don't know, slut-face, how about the truth? Anyways, it turned out it had been happening for a while before we broke up and I was naturally furious with both of them. Not that I'm sad (any more) about breaking up with her, but I was disappointed they had to do it so badly and basically rule out the option of me being mates with them.

Now, ideally this sort of thing happens and you never see them again but unfortunately we share the same group of friends. Our friends made life for them pretty awful for a few months but I always knew they'd be back in the good books with everyone sooner or later. So this presented a problem for me. I was going to have to be around them sometimes - ie friend's birthdays, engagement parties.

I went to a mate's wedding in Colorado and the girlfriend-stealing cocksucker was the best man. When I arrived in town my mates took me out on a tour of all the bars and he kept trying to offer me drinks. I told him to keep his distance for the week and there'd be no problems. He didn't give up. Now keeping in

Sex and Friendship

mind I'd been travelling for 40 hours and was 10,000 feet above sea level (I live about 20 feet above sea level in Sydney), I got super pissed that night. I can't remember the details but I do remember punching him in the face a couple of times. I wish I could remember more because maybe then I'd feel like I got payback or something. Instead it feels really hollow and pretty shameful.

Anyway, the bottom line is now it's over a year since it all happened and I've been seeing them a fair bit. I was best man in a different wedding and my ex-girlfriend was my corresponding bridesmaid so we were thrown together for photos. Smile! Also, I spent the weekend with dicknut when we were on the stag party for the same wedding. It was actually OK, and we spoke and had a bit of a laugh. It's strange how time can sort that shit out. It'll never be the same though, and at this stage I only see them when circumstance makes it happen. Who knows if that will change?

Even if you don't go after your friend's partner, problems can still arise: namely, when a friend's partner comes on to you. This is most people's worst nightmare — you risk hurting your mate, or worse, losing them, if you tell them what's happened. But if you don't tell them they'll carry on dating a loser who'd come on to their friends.

You Must Be My Best Friend ...

Darlene's story: He made his move

My best friend had been dating a married man for several months. She hadn't realised that he was married when they met, but as soon as she did, I warned her to get out. He'd do it to her. She seemed to believe that it was true love, but I didn't trust him at all.

Sure enough, the first time that I met him, I thought he was slimy. He kept belittling her, and hated it when he wasn't the centre of attention. When my friend went to the loo, he leaned over, put his hand on my knee, then whispered, 'You're so cute,' in my ear. He started stroking my thigh, so I just moved away in disgust. When my friend came back, I pretended nothing had happened – I didn't want to sour the evening. But the next day, I gave her a call, explained what had happened and, thank God, she believed me. She thanked me for telling her and hung up.

The next time I saw her, she told me that she'd challenged him about it and he'd said it was an innocent mistake – he was being friendly and I must have misconstrued it. She said that she wasn't annoyed with me but that I should be more careful about the way I saw things.

I was frustrated that she took his word over mine, but decided to let it lie. She wanted to believe that her boyfriend was Mr Perfect, and no amount of warnings were going to stop her. I was relieved when they broke up a few months later though – I didn't want her getting hurt by a man like that.

Sex and Friendship

Different Attitudes to Sex

And finally, there's one more way that sex can affect friendship. If your friend has a different attitude to sex than you do then this can lead to conflict. Say, for example, your knickers are up and down more than an elevator, while your friend is saving herself until she gets married. This may not be a problem if both of you respect the other one's opinion. If, however, you call her frigid and she thinks you're a slut, you're going to end up in a lot of rows.

'Live and let live' is the best attitude to have. After all, what suits one person may well be another one's idea of hell. So rather than judging each other, learn from each other's attitudes and experiences. Sexual expression is different for everyone and there are benefits and pitfalls to every different kind of lifestyle. It's entirely possible to be friends with someone who sees sex in a very different way to you – just look at an episode of *Sex and the City* to see how.

Failing that, just avoid talking about sex altogether – or find friends who have a similar attitude to sex as you do.

Magnolia's story: She was too uptight

Twenty-some-odd years ago I was friends (well, friends-ish) with Cindy Lou. Cindy Lou and I decided to take a weekend

You Must Be My Best Friend ...

trip to Montreal one January, as the rates were low. Well, the snow was up to our asses and the temperature well below zero, so why wouldn't they be?

As behooves all young women heading to Montreal on a train, we got drunk on Amaretto with some hockey players we met. So far, all is well. I think to myself, 'Hey, Cindy Lou is a lot of fun.' After discarding our fellow travellers and sobering up some, we headed out into a miserable night to have a good time. We dined on French food, shopped for boots, and met up with a group of attractive young men. One of these young men looked like Jim Morrison (the young, slinky-hipped Jim, not the bloated Jim) so, of course, I was all over him like a silly metaphor on a dolt.

The group of us (including Cindy Lou) went to this club and that, getting thrown out hither and yon, until the yawningly late hour of 11pm, whereupon Cindy Lou commenced nagging and whining at me to go back to the hotel. I dug my soddenly drunken heels in and refused to go. I was young, attractive, drunk, travelling *sans* parents for the first time, and clinging to young Jim. She muttered her solo way to bed while I continued my merrymaking, eventually ending up in a pay-by-the-hour dive somewhere near Place Ville-Marie. We ... well, you know what we did ... until dawn's early light.

I staggered my way back to our hotel, and returned to our room at about 6am. Cindy Lou woke up hangover-free and started with the nagging again. She then used my semi-drunken, semi-hung over state to force me on a bus tour of Montreal churches.

Sex and Friendship

A few months later she told me I was getting fat, so I slept with her boyfriend. I haven't seen her since.

Looking back at this, I know I'm coming across as something of a sociopathic trollop, but you can only understand the level of poor conduct inspired by the self-righteous, humourless, Lutheran manner of a Cindy Lou if you actually spend some time with a Cindy Lou. I have kept my life free of Cindy Lou and all Cindy Lou types since that time, and am much the healthier for it.

* * *

When it comes down to it, sex is complex and friendships are complex, so it's hardly surprising that the two can collide in numerous ways. However, by working to keep the balance right so that you're putting as much effort into your friendships as you do into getting laid – if not more – then you should be able to negotiate most issues.

TEN WAYS TO STOP SEX AFFECTING YOUR FRIENDSHIPS

1. Agree ground-rules before you go out on the pull with a friend.
2. Don't make a move on a friend unless you're damn sure that they feel the same way.

You Must Be My Best Friend ...

3. Expect to lose some mutual friends when you split up from a long-term partner.
4. Never flirt with a friend who fancies you if the feeling isn't mutual — it's unfair leading someone on.
5. Remember the three-month rule: for the first three months of a relationship, your friend is off her head on naturally produced chemicals, so cut her a bit of slack if she's a rubbish pal for a while.
6. Try to befriend your pal's partner if they are jealous of you.
7. Never cop off with a friend's partner ... but if you do, expect the friendship to end should they ever find out.
8. If you want to stay friends with an ex, take a break from seeing each other for at least a fortnight first.
9. Only talk about your sex life with friends who are open to listening to you ...
10. ... and don't be judgemental of friends who have different sexual lifestyles to you.

Chapter Six

In It for the Long Haul

If you've managed to negotiate your way through all the pitfalls so far, well done. But don't think you're home and dry quite yet. There are still a myriad of other things that can go wrong.

You'd think that friendship would get easier the longer you know someone. If you've got a shared history going back years, you've probably got a good idea of how to deal with each other. And while this can be true, long-term friendships can also bring new problems to the fore.

The longer you know someone, the more likely certain things become, like going on holiday together or living together. And on a more worrying note, the better you know someone, the more likely you are to notice if they have a dangerous pattern of behaviour, whether it's repeatedly making the same mistakes with relationships and work, or developing some kind of dependency to, say, drugs or alcohol.

All of these things can be dealt with, in some cases with help from professionals, but they add up to mean that long-term friendships can be far from easy. Maintaining a friendship takes just as much work as forming one in the first place — if not more. But if you can work through these things with your friend it will make your relationship much richer and stronger.

WE'RE ALL GOING ON A SUMMER HOLIDAY

If you're friends with someone for years, at some stage you'll probably think that going on holiday with them would be a good idea. While holidaying with friends can be brilliant fun, it can also bring all-new conflicts to the surface. Different people want different things from their vacation, and people tend to be precious about the time that they spend away from work, because most of us get such limited holiday allowance, time-wise, and taking a break can be an expensive business.

If a friend suggests that you join her for a holiday to a destination that you hate the idea of, for God's sake don't go. You may want to spend time with your friend but you'll only resent it if you end up wasting your time off work going somewhere that leaves you cold. And chances are, what with you being human and everything, you'll take this out on your friend.

Assuming that you share similar tastes in destination, before you commit to a fortnight in the sun, week in a chalet or month trekking on safari together, it's still worth taking a weekend break somewhere closer to home first. Getting

In It for the Long Haul

through a weekend is easy enough if you're good friends, but it will also throw up any potential conflicts. For example, some people like getting up early in the morning when they're on holiday to take advantage of every moment that they're away, while others see it as a chance to escape from their alarm clock. If you're going on an activity holiday together, differing levels of fitness can have an impact: one of you may feel like they're being left behind, while another feels like they're being held up. You may be the kind of person who loves wandering round all the tourist attractions, while your friend might prefer 'going native' and seeing how people in the area really live. And if one of you is single but the other one is attached, it could lead to problems, if you want to go out on the pull but your friend wants to have a quiet dinner talking to you.

All of these things can be easy enough to cope with over a couple of days but if you have different approaches to what you're after, it suggests that a longer break could lead to big rows. So save your holiday plans for people who share the same preferences as you.

It also makes sense if you go on holiday with people who have a similar budget to you. Neither of you will have much fun if there's a major disparity between what you can afford. The richer friend will resent having to slum it and the poorer friend will feel insecure or guilty about being unable to enjoy the good life.

You Must Be My Best Friend ...

Amma's story: Holiday hell

When I was in my first year at university, I made friends with Joanna. She was always the centre of attention whenever we went out, but I liked being with her. There was something about being surrounded by people hanging off her every word that made me feel like I belonged too. So when her dad offered to pay for us to go on holiday together, I was over the moon. I couldn't afford a holiday because I was scraping it together on a student grant, but her parents were loaded and she always had money to spare because they spoiled her rotten.

She and I spent ages deciding where we'd go together, and settled on a Greek island. Her dad made it very clear that the money he gave her was for both of us and that I shouldn't feel bad about it – it was a present for us both.

When we arrived at the hotel, Joanna instantly picked the bed with a sea view. I thought that it was fair enough as her dad had paid for the holiday. It wasn't until we got to dinner that we ran into any problems. She ordered a full three-course meal for herself and then said, 'What are you having? The omelette looks good.' She'd deliberately picked the cheapest thing on the menu for me, and when I said I liked the idea of the tuna, she said, 'That's a bit dear – pick something else.' She strongly intimated that I'd be taking the piss if I wanted a starter or dessert. I watched her enjoy her three-course meal while I had to make do with egg and chips (the second cheapest thing on the menu).

In It for the Long Haul

As the week progressed, she just got worse. Every meal was the same – she'd have the most expensive thing on the menu and would direct me to have the cheapest thing. Every penny that she spent on me was grudging. I know her dad was paying, but that was the only way I could afford to go, and I'd made it clear that I was happy to go to a cheaper destination and pay my own way – she just didn't want to go somewhere cheap.

By the end of the week, I felt like her poor relative – and she still made me feel like I was being demanding every time I asked for anything, even a drink of water when it was 92 degrees. The money situation dictated our entire holiday and when I got back, it took me a while to forget how she'd treated me. In hindsight, I wish I'd dumped her immediately after the holiday though – she ended up stealing my boyfriend. Clearly, her attitude was what was hers, she kept, but what was mine, was fair game.

If there are big differences between what you and your friend want on holiday, but you still want to enjoy escaping your normal lives together, it can be worth considering going on holiday with a group of friends, with some who share her interests and some who share yours. Unless you really can't avoid it, never go on holiday as a threesome. If you do, you can guarantee that one person will always feel left out, which doesn't make for a fun time. And it should be taken as read

You Must Be My Best Friend ...

that, for a group holiday, you pick people who get on with each other. If you're thinking about inviting someone your other friends don't know that well, spend a night out together first to see how well the group gels. Nothing is worse than getting away together only to discover a major personality clash between one or more of the people you're trapped with for your holiday.

Deborah's story: A disastrous week away

My partner, Ben, and I went to Italy last summer with a friend of ours, Linda, and stayed in her parents' villa outside Majorca. Originally there was meant to be a large group of us going but it ended up being just Ben, Linda, her friend Alison and me. The holiday was a disaster from start to finish.

We'd pre-booked a hire car for the two weeks and at Linda's request added Ben as a named driver. Once we arrived in Spain, she said she didn't feel comfortable driving abroad (something she hadn't realised when she went through the booking process online in England that automatically classed her as the driver since she was the person booking).

Driving from the airport to the villa we got lost, as she'd never been there before. It became very apparent on the journey just how scared she was of her father. She refused to call him and ask for further directions because she kept saying, 'He'll kill me, he'll have a go at me for being so stupid that I can't find the place.' She was genuinely petrified of admitting to her dad that she couldn't do something - like she'd let him down. Anyway, eventually she had to call him and she ended up in tears on the phone, but we managed to find the villa at long last.

Once inside the villa she became the control freak from hell. She was incredibly bossy and very protective of the villa. We all felt like she was treating us like three-year-olds and resented many of her comments, as - believe it or not - we do all own houses and know what to do/what not to do around the home. She panicked every time one of us opened a cupboard (in case we damaged it) or when we got glasses/crockery out of the cupboard to use. OK, the villa was very posh and full of expensive furniture, but this still didn't change the fact that we are all responsible adults and knew how to behave without being told what to do.

Whenever we made plans we had to do what she wanted to do. It was as if we all owed her something due to the fact that we were staying in her parents' villa and she therefore had the right to run the holiday. On days when we did something that one of us had suggested rather than her, she walked round with a face like a slapped arse and made it clear she was not enjoying herself because she didn't get her own way!

Ben did all the cooking (as he loves cooking) but even then, she had to try and boss him around each time we went to the supermarket and dictate what he was to buy and to cook, even to the extent that she made comments like: 'I'm looking forward

You Must Be My Best Friend ...

to this as I had an input'. She was then clearly put out when Ben had ignored her and done his own thing anyway.

I've known this friend for seven years and thought she was a good friend. But if all her controlling and bossiness wasn't bad enough, this gets worse. Linda is very tall and skinny and, quite frankly, knows she's very attractive. I, on the other hand, am not ugly by any means but I have always struggled with my weight. A few months before the holiday I injured my shoulder and had to stop my kickboxing for a while. During this time, I had put on weight and was very frustrated with it all. For the entire two weeks of the holiday, Linda kept making comments about my size and about how much I was eating. Once, when I was offered some more lasagne and I was considering it, Linda looked straight at me and said, 'No, you've had enough.' Also, when I was talking to Alison about a patch of broken veins on my leg, I said, 'I've had them for years – I don't know what to do about them,' and Linda said, 'Lose weight'. On another occasion, I took a handful of crisps from the bag she was offering round (which I'd actually bought!) and she said, 'Have you got enough?' There were other digs too but I can't remember them all.

I should have said something to her after the first comment but frankly I was so shocked that I didn't and then it made it harder with each comment that followed. I dealt with it by ignoring her/not talking to her and being really grumpy with her, which in hindsight didn't help anyone, as she obviously didn't have a clue why I was off with her and the others had to

In It for the Long Haul

deal with my mood. Thankfully her friend Alison was sick of her also and we escaped for walks while Ben was cooking! Not once did Linda ever make a nasty comment in front of Ben, as she knew damn well she would have received a mouthful from him.

Eventually Ben had words with her in Italy as my mood was frustrating him. She said she'd never deliberately hurt me and didn't realise her comments were being taken like that. He told her to think before she spoke.

Things didn't get any better once we returned home; I wanted nothing to do with her, and it was a long while before I could see her. We are 'OK' now but have only seen each other a handful of times since July last year as I can't be bothered with her now. I saw a different side to her that I didn't like and I will never treat her as a close friend again.

If you go on holiday with a friend and it starts to go pear-shaped, nip it in the bud as quickly as possible. This is not a time to be stubborn. If you've done something that's offended your friend, apologise — even if it wasn't your fault and she just took something you said out of context. And if she's the one that said something wrong, don't dwell on it. Say that it upset you but then move on; there's no point both of you having a lousy time on holiday, and if it's a major issue, you can always go over it once you get home.

You Must Be My Best Friend ...

Amy's story: Honesty is the best policy

I've been on holiday with my best mate, Lucy, a couple of times and both times have been fantastic. She and I have known each other for three years and it's safe to say that we've talked about every aspect of our lives. However, there's a ten-year age gap between us so I was a bit nervous the first time we went away together. Even though she parties just as hard as I do, we don't see each other that often and I thought that she might need to take more breaks between nights out than I did.

I couldn't have been more wrong. If anything, she was the one encouraging me to go wild. There were a couple of times that could have been problematic – once when a bloke I fancied came on to her and once when we both fell in lust with the same barman – but we got over it easily enough. In the first case, she made sure that I was involved in the conversation but, once it became clear that he really wasn't interested in me, I told her (in the loos, obviously) that I was fine with her going for it. In return, she let me have the barman.

We also had a long discussion before we went away. Even though the aim of the holiday was to have a bit of an adventure and go wild, we both admitted we needed time to ourselves. Because we'd talked about it beforehand, it meant that neither of us thought that we'd done anything wrong when the other one decided to stay in and read a book, or go off wandering alone.

Lucy is my favourite person in the world and going on holiday has only brought us closer. When we get back from holiday, we always have a break from seeing each other for about a week, so that we don't get bored of each other, but the following week we're usually talking about hitting the travel agents and deciding where to go for our next trip.

HOME SWEET HELL

If you get on with a friend really well, you might even consider moving in with them. This isn't just something that affects students nowadays. With rising house prices, there's an increase in the number of friends who are pooling their income in order to get on the housing ladder, and nowadays there are even special mortgages available for friends.

It should go without saying that if you're considering buying a house or apartment with a friend that you should rent somewhere together for at least three months – ideally six – first. The last thing that you want is to get financially tied to someone who you realise later is impossible to live with.

Before you move in with a friend, make sure that you know exactly what they're like with money. This is often the root cause of the biggest rows when you're living with someone: you may want to pay the bills as soon as they come in, while your friend is more of the 'leave it until the bailiffs are knocking on the door' mentality. An easy way to find out how financially organised someone is, is to ask if they know their current bank balance. (Don't ask them how much it is as some people don't

You Must Be My Best Friend ...

like sharing financial information — just ask if they know roughly how much cash they have.) If not, be warned, you could be dealing with a financial flake.

Conversely, if you're the person who's rubbish with money, make sure you set up direct debits with your bank so that all the bills are paid on time. Friendship is too important to risk just because you can't get your act together. Get into the habit of writing down all the money that you spend so that you can avoid the horror of going to the cash machine and avoiding looking at the balance — or worse, assuming that you have lots of money in your account, spending it all, then realising that you've spent that month's rent/mortgage.

You should also consider whether your lifestyle is all that similar to your friend's. If you're into having big parties every weekend but your friend prefers a quieter life, it's probably best that you avoid living together no matter how well you get on with each other. When you're living together the smallest things can really wind you up. Cleaning and tidying are often seen as minor issues but they can become all-encompassing when you share accommodation if you have different standards to your mates. One person's 'tidy' flat could be another's mould-ridden hell hole, so check out the state of your pal's current flat and show them yours — as it really is, rather than preparing it for guests. If you cringe because their magazines aren't at right angles on the coffee table, or they look disgusted because you haven't done last night's washing up, you're heading for trouble. It's not insoluble — a rota or hiring a cleaner can both deal with the issue – but agree before you move in. Afterwards, it'll be to late and the damage to the friendship will already be done.

Even the smallest things should be agreed before you move in. Set out ground rules about going into each other's rooms (should you knock first?), borrowing each other's food or clothes, having people to stay the night (or longer), remembering to double-lock the doors at night, decorating communal areas, how the bills will be divided and even using up the hot water. And it may sound stupid, but before you commit to living with someone, it's worth considering whether you share the same taste in home furnishings. Spending time in your friend's kitsch bedroom is all very well, but when you're sharing the same space, it will drive you up the wall if she wants to paint the place orange and tiger-striped when you're into a more classic look. You need to have a pretty strong friendship to survive even the most seemingly trivial of problems when you live together, so take nothing for granted.

And of course, you should make sure that your friend is sane. Otherwise things can go horribly wrong …

Marcelle's story: The friend who became the lodger from hell

When I first met Nate admittedly I was not on my best behaviour. It was in the middle of a pregnancy scare and I'd arranged

You Must Be My Best Friend ...

to meet a Significant Other in a bar, to discuss what to do. That guy, being a bit of a plonker, had invited Nate along as a diversion strategy. Within the hour, I'd tipped a full pint of beer over Matt's head with Nate in a ringside seat. Of course, being a mad load of horror fans, such behaviour is considered feisty and inspirational, and we left Nate smiling to himself as we were thrown out, screaming, into the street.

A few months later, I ended up sitting next to Nate on a flight to Montreal. Matt had conveniently dumped me just before we were off on a press jaunt for two weeks. Nate was about ten years older than me, infinitely more experienced as a journo in the field, but he wasn't stuck up. He was one of those people that you could just sit and talk to for hours and hours and never even notice the time.

Nate progressed to the role of official confidant, and had no hesitation in agreeing to rent a room in my house when I needed a lodger. Nate settled in quickly, although I thought it was strange that he brought almost nothing with him. Where was the prized video collection I was longing to get a look at? For weeks he gave me a running story - it had all been loaded into a van, the axels of which broke. It was at a mate's house, and the mate was now on holiday. Funnily enough, the big moving-in day never emerged, but I noticed that bits and pieces kept turning up piecemeal.

After a few months it became pretty clear he was an alcoholic. His career was also suspect. He worked one day a week in a speciality film shop and did a few reviews every

In It for the Long Haul

month for a film magazine, but beyond that there was nothing steady or solid, hardly enough to generate the cash for a man who partied every night. It was a mystery how he paid the rent, and, as the months went by he became more tardy with the rent.

Unfortunately, the later he was with the rent, the more he avoided me. He put a lock on his door and refused to answer or come out if I left a couple of messages for him. It was exasperating because I hadn't done anything wrong, and the full mortgage, if I had to pay it by myself, was almost my month's take-home salary. A third lodger, Maria, arrived and the rent decreased accordingly. Nate seemed to resent Maria's presence, but as he'd had so many financial problems it seemed more sensible to let her stay.

During this time I had no steady partner and was involved in a number of gossamer-thin relationships. On the rare occasions when I dragged someone back to my lair, Nate could be relied upon to behave badly. In fact, he gave the impression he was my husband or ex-partner from the look on his sorrowful face. He just couldn't cope with me getting involved with anyone else, apart from Matt. (The irony being that Matt was probably the most unsuitable man for me in London.) At the same time, lots of things that should have arrived in the post (Valentine's cards, photos, letters) never turned up and people kept asking if I'd received a particular phone message which I never got. It took me months to work out that Nate must have been deleting them. In fact, looking

You Must Be My Best Friend ...

for one of my CDs in his room, I found one of the missing photographs that had got 'lost in the post' covered with dirty heel marks. It was so obvious, I should have cottoned on earlier; Nate couldn't stand me being involved with anyone else, and so he'd been sabotaging my relationships. It was the last straw.

By this time, his alcoholism was in full swing and he was on a downward spiral. He was later than ever with the rent, and I'd taken to writing him letters asking him to move out. Every time I tried to speak to him he just shut himself up in his room. It was ridiculous! On one occasion I'd waited up until 3.30am to speak to him and then we'd had a fight in the kitchen, I pushed Nate and he fell into a glass door, which broke. Although he was unhurt, Maria had been so terrified by the commotion that she moved out the next day.

Still he would not leave. I'd tried writing letters and even got some legal advice. Although he had no legal rights to be there if I no longer wanted it (it was my house), physically getting him out was another thing. It became evident that this was what he had done before, running up debts and then refusing to pay up, hence his cloak-and-dagger lifestyle. By this time, all the good things we'd had in our friendship had evaporated. I was finding him drunk, sprawled out on the stairs, and his room was beginning to stink of old clothes and dried alcohol. He'd spilled a lot of vodka all over the light-coloured carpet and dozens of newspapers had been pressed into it, leaving black marks. By now I was past caring, I just wanted him out and gone.

In It for the Long Haul

Eventually, about nine months after I'd first asked him, Nate moved out. He didn't say anything to me, but just upped and went. He left most of his things in the garden shed, and he walked mud around the whole house shifting his things. He also left the back door open and managed to shut the next-door neighbour's cat in my room! Of course, he didn't pay the back rent he owed, although an unexpected letter from his parents offered to pay anything I was due.

I met his parents some months later and it turned out that they had been giving him the rent money for my place all along. They also asked if I'd take him back if they paid me direct, but I refused. We'd had so much in common and the good side of him was a wonderful person, but it was his erratic mean streak that I couldn't be doing with.

* * *

You'd think that living with someone who makes your life hell or being trapped on holiday with someone you can't stand would be about as bad as things can get. But, sadly, not all friendship problems are sorted with practice runs, a simple apology or by dealing with insecurities. Being someone's friend also means that you might be exposed to more serious issues in their life; recognising that they have an addiction, a mental illness or are facing domestic violence at home. While it's worth seeking advice from specialists in the area should you encounter this, it's worth having an outline of what you should do should you have to deal with a serious problem.

DEALING WITH A FRIEND'S ADDICTIONS

Most people have some vice or another: smoking, drinking or even just caffeine. And while it would be great (if a little boring) if we could all be dead virtuous and look after our bodies, bad habits are part of life. However, there's a difference between a habit and an addiction, and it's often easier to see things escalating in a friend than it is to identify it in yourself.

If a friend of yours suddenly starts being late all the time, it can suggest there's a problem, particularly if their lateness starts to affect their job or other 'important' things. Obviously, lateness doesn't always indicate an addiction – some people are just naturally bad at timekeeping, but if someone's always been punctual before, it can indicate there might be something wrong.

Another thing to watch out for is a friend suddenly having difficulties performing their job or socialising because they're constantly on a comedown, hung over or have 'the shakes'. If this is the case, you may need to intervene – particularly if they don't see it a problem because they can easily fix it with another drink/line of coke/spliff. Other physical signs to watch out for are headaches, blackouts, swollen ankles or sudden weight loss.

In It for the Long Haul

Addiction can also affect mood, so if your friend becomes more irritable or suddenly starts rowing more often with you, their family or their other half, then keep an eye out. Even 'positive' personality changes can be an early warning sign: a friend who's shy might become much more extrovert when they're drinking, and rely on it to provide confidence; or if they are only relaxed after a spliff, they may be too dependent.

People with addictions tend to use their vice of choice to deal with personal troubles or fears. The addiction is rarely the problem: it's the addict's inability to handle the other difficulties they face in life that is the major issue. Their dependency comes from trying to escape the way they feel.

If you suspect a friend is suffering from an addiction, you'll probably want to wade in to fix the situation. It can be frustrating watching someone that you care about turn into an addict, so you may be tempted to get all heavy-handed, but don't. Make sure you avoid making threats ('I'll stop being your friend unless you sort it out.') or going for direct action, like hiding all the alcohol in their house or locking them up – that's removing the choice from their hands, so isn't helpful. And, while it may seem like a natural solution, keeping your friend away from people who are 'bad influences' (eg her drug dealer/drinking buddies) is counter-productive because your friend needs to learn how to handle their addiction, rather than just avoid it. That said, arranging nights out that don't revolve around their drink/drug of choice is helpful, and will help show them it's possible to have fun without being intoxicated.

You Must Be My Best Friend ...

You may want to reason with your friend, and find out why they're turning to drink/drugs, but this can backfire because, often, the addict doesn't know what their problem is either. It may sound overly negative, but dealing with an addict really does need professional help, and if you try to solve the problem, you'll just end up feeling like a failure and might even push your friend away. What you can do is encourage your friend towards seeking that help, be it a doctor or support group (see Useful Resources). Chances are, she won't think she has a problem — as is often said: the first step to recovery is admitting that you have a problem — but you'll have a better chance of getting through if you ask your friend about it when they're sober/not high. Tell your friend how their addictive behaviour affects you, and let them know what it's like dealing with them when they're under the influence.

Even if your friend won't listen, you can get help for yourself by seeking counselling. It may seem like an overreaction, but dealing with an addict is stressful too, so make sure that you get support if you need it.

Jemima's story: Drug-fuelled fun turned sour

Sam was one of the first people I met when I went to university. We lived in the same halls and spent our first year doing everything but studying. In fact we barely even made it onto campus. We had a club night for every evening of the week and they

In It for the Long Haul

would invariably end up in a big old speed- and pill-fuelled mash-up. We were real partners in crime and at the end of the first year we moved into a teeny flat above a shop, right in the middle of town. We furnished it by nicking stuff from skips and decorated it with rows of empty booze bottles.

When the new term started I got a bit more involved with school, I had a new boyfriend and some new uni friends, and Sam was working full-time in a clothes shop. One night she was sitting on the windowsill in her bedroom watching the Saturday night buzz when she spotted a guy on his own. She shouted after him and asked where he was going. He said he was off to a free party and did she want to come? They became a couple and he started hanging round our house a lot. I didn't like him from the start and I told her, but she was, and still is, a right stubborn pain in the arse and wouldn't have any of it. We started going out together a bit less and she started seeing more of Andy.

One morning she came into my room and woke me up. I was hung over and blurry and she said, 'Mate, wake up, I have to tell you something. Last night I smoked heroin.' I told her to get out my room, I didn't want to talk to her. She tried to explain that it wasn't bad, it was a chilled-out social thing, like smoking a spliff, but I was so angry I wouldn't listen.

And that was the beginning of a long nightmare. Everything just spiralled out of control. I wouldn't listen, she wanted to talk. I told all our straighter friends what she had done and she was furious. Our house, which had always been full of noise and the

You Must Be My Best Friend ...

place everyone ended up, became a war zone with each of us listening for the other's footsteps so as to avoid each other in the hallway. After a while she promised me she wouldn't do it any more and we tried to get things back on track. About a week after her promise I went into her room to borrow a CD and found a small pile of burnt foil on the floor.

We had always taken heaps of drugs together so there is no way I can moralise about the situation. I can't say heroin is evil yet cram handfuls of pills down my throat at the weekend, but people had died, people were so ill you could look right through their gaunt eyes and find nothing in them, people were lying, stealing, whoring and we had seen it all and why would you want to get involved with that? I told her I didn't want to live with a junkie, I didn't want heroin in my house and I didn't want her in my house.

There was a lot of rowing and shouting and door slamming. In reality, all I wanted was for her to stop seeing that horrible guy and to be my Sam again but all that ever came out my mouth was nasty and abusive and completely unhelpful.

Almost two years later she phoned me and said she needed somewhere to crash for a weekend while they were in between homes. I asked if Andy was still using and she said no, so I agreed to have them over. It was so good to see her again but two days predictably turned into three, then four, and then one morning I overheard her crying because she couldn't find a vein. After she went to work I went into the bathroom and found blood everywhere. I was so sad I didn't know what to do. More than anything I was sad that she was lying to me, that this amazing, beautiful, intelligent, witty, sexy, brilliant girl was fucking up so badly, and that we had been so close and now she had to lie to me. When she came in from work I sat her down and told her she had to go. She started crying, telling me they had nowhere to go and she would get help, that I could help her get help. I couldn't believe that someone who had so much originality and charisma had turned into such a cliché. I made them leave there and then and watched as they trundled a shopping trolley full of their possessions down the street.

We didn't talk at all after that. She lived in a squat for about six months and then Andy suddenly went overseas. I don't know what happened to her then but she eventually went back to her parents' house in her home town and went cold turkey in her bedroom without them ever finding out. I thought about her a lot, I still missed her even though we hadn't been friends for a long time. I had finished my degree, got a job, done all those grown-up things and one day someone said they had bumped into her and she was looking really well. That afternoon I sent her a CD single of the song we always used to listen to before we went out, with a silly note on it with my mobile number and email address on it, but I didn't really expect to hear back from her. Two days later she called. She told me she was so sorry for everything and she loved me. She was clean, she had a job, a boyfriend and was going to train to be a drugs counsellor.

Now, we live on opposite sides of the country but we talk every week, email and text, and we see each other as often as possible. She's always the one I call to bitch about my crazy flatmate and she always calls me on Sundays to blether crap at me when she's recovering from her weekends. She's fit and healthy and alive. She's engaged to a really top guy, she's a drugs counsellor who doesn't judge or condemn and she's really happy.

There wasn't any obvious reason why she started using but I think I understand. I can't ever think less of her because of it. I have so much respect for her strength in overcoming it and she always tells me she admires my tenacity and drive. Sometimes I can barely believe that after all those years of proper sex, drugs and rock 'n' rolling that we are still such good friends.

DEALING WITH DEPRESSION

About a third of people suffer from some form of mental illness in their life, so it's pretty likely that you'll encounter a friend with psychological issues at some point, depression being one of the most common (eating disorders are also increasingly common – but usually have the same root cause: low self-esteem). And, as a friend, you may find it easier to spot than the person who's actually ill.

Things to watch out for include your friend spending hours in bed (alone – just because your best friend gets a stud who keeps her at it for hours, it doesn't mean she's depressed – in fact she's probably quite the opposite), a radical change of lifestyle, loss of energy, insomnia and sudden weight gain or loss. And if your pal suddenly stops being nice to be near because they're getting stinky, forgets important occasions or spends all their time procrastinating rather than actually doing anything, don't just think they're being thoughtless or lazy: all these things can be warning signs too.

A depressive may get obsessed with something or someone who's bad for them, or develop a compulsion to do something to excess. (NB: you're looking for changes in behaviour here. If a friend of yours always dates guys who are bad news or has always partied hard, it's less of a sign — though it may still be worth them seeking counselling as they're exhibiting negative behaviours.) And if a friend suddenly starts alienating you or other friends and family — by being bitchy, dismissive, blaming all their problems on you or generally behaving in an unpleasant way — it can also suggest that things aren't as they should be.

Depressives will frequently withdraw from life, losing interest in work or their education, and forgoing social events. And in some cases, they may also self-harm, so watch out for marks on their body — scratches, bruises or other wounds.

Other symptoms of depression include asking for advice when the answer seems obvious, and making negative comments (which may be masked as dark humour) like 'life isn't worth living' or 'I'm useless', or defeatist comments like, 'I'm never going to have any luck.' Someone who's had a strong sense of faith may lose theirs, and generally, a depressive will see everything in the most negative way.

You Must Be My Best Friend ...

Mania is also a relatively common disorder. Signs a friend may suffer from it include them being very up one day and down the next, beginning lots of unrealistic projects (often 'get rich quick') but never completing them, and being hyper with little need for sleep. They may go on shopping trips when they're absurdly broke (then again, don't we all?), blurt out inappropriate and badly timed comments (ditto) or frequently change their opinion on things – say, one day hating a political party and the next day raving about it.

Someone who is depressed or manic may get suicidal. While a person who is suicidal undoubtedly needs professional help, you can watch for the warning signs so that you can encourage your friend to seek help. If your friend starts giving away important possessions, suddenly gets calm or focused despite being in a midst of problems, talks about people who have died as being lucky, seems to see no hope for change in the future or simply gives up on communicating then they could be at risk.

People can turn suicidal for all manner of reasons. It could be because they have a depressive/suicidal history and are facing a new crisis, or going through something 'final' like graduating, finishing a job or their children leaving home. Health problems can lead some people to become depressed and/or suicidal. And if your depressed friend encounters things that could count as 'the last straw' in a marriage, job, financial objective or a life-long dream, this could also trigger suicidal thoughts. Most of these things, when witnessed alone, don't definitely mean that a person is depressed. However, if someone has several symptoms, it's worthy of concern.

When it comes to dealing with a depressive, bear in mind that you shouldn't attempt to take the place of a GP or counsellor. You should also be aware that dealing with a depressed friend is bloody hard work. It can be draining, stressful and bring you down, so only give as much support as you are able to while still clinging on to your own sanity. Don't try to become your friend's therapist and get to the root of the issue, but do support and encourage them. Low self-esteem feeds into depression, so remind them, subtly, of how fantastic they are, and let them know that you care about them.

You might think that you can take a back seat should your friend start seeing a counsellor, but they'll still need reassurance that they are liked, even once they're getting treatment. The same goes if they start taking medication. Depression can take a long time to treat so don't expect your friend to get better overnight just because they are on the path to solving the problem. It's not that easy.

If your friend is depressed, it can be tempting to try to run their life, by making doctor's appointments for them or arranging a counsellor for them to help their problems go away. However, this can be counter-productive, as the depressive needs to admit they have a problem and take those steps themselves. Offering to go with them to their appointment once they've taken that step can be helpful, and doesn't take the responsibility from their hands – but don't insist, as they

You Must Be My Best Friend ...

may not need it. Similarly, if your friend lies in bed all the time, taking them round the occasional meal is OK but don't get into a habit of doing it, as they may come to depend on you, and sink further into their illness.

The main role you have as the depressive's friend is to help them realise that they are depressed — and that it's the depression which is the problem, not them. Never say things like 'cheer up' or 'things are bound to get better, there's no need to get into a state', because your friend won't be able to see it like that. They can't just switch 'happy' back on in their head — hard as it may be to understand, the depression is there thanks to brain chemistry, not just getting a bit glum.

Instead, listen to your friend, and help boost their confidence. Encourage them to keep up their therapy/medication, and keep an eye on them to see whether they're getting any better. It usually takes a couple of weeks for most antidepressants to kick in, but after that point, there should start to be an improvement — however mild — in their state. If not, recommend that they get back to the professionals. It's important to remember that depression isn't purely a situational thing; it's down to a complex hybrid of chemicals and is just as much of an illness as flu.

If someone you know dies through suicide, you may want to blame yourself but, much as you wouldn't blame yourself if a friend died of cancer, you need to realise that the depressive was ill and it was the illness that killed them. No matter how much you try to help your friend, at the end of the day, only one

In It for the Long Haul

person can fix a depressive and that's the individual who suffers with the disease. So if the illness ends up being terminal to them, it may sound harsh, but it's absolutely not your fault. It's worth seeking counselling yourself to help you through this time too, as it can be a hard thing to go through alone.

Jo's story: We're friends but it's hard

I've known Flora for years and she's always been very up and down. When I first met her, I thought that she was an extrovert. She was always the life and soul of the party and generally surrounded by a group of people hanging off her every word. She's got a wicked sense of humour and is one of those people who knows everyone. I've got to admit, when we first met each other, I was a bit jealous. But as I got to know her better, I realised that was only one side of her personality.

One night, I went round to see Flora - we were supposed to be meeting up with a group of friends for dinner and she lives near me so decided to go together. When I turned up, she looked really upset - her eyes were red and she looked like she'd been crying. She tried to smile, and when I asked her what was wrong, she said that there wasn't any problem - she just wasn't in the mood for going out. I managed to talk her round but she was subdued all evening.

Over the next couple of years, there were a few instances like this. She wouldn't be her usual bubbly self. But I didn't think

You Must Be My Best Friend ...

that there was anything serious going on – until she split up with Ahmed, her long-term partner. I went round to see her, as you do, expecting a night of crying and man-bashing, and armed with tissues. Instead, she was really quiet. She hardly spoke to me and in the end, I asked her if she'd rather be alone. She said yes. The next day, I got a call from a mutual friend who was in tears. Apparently, Fiona had taken an overdose after I'd left and was rushed to hospital to have her stomach pumped. I was horrified – even when I found out that she was OK. Surely I could have done something to stop her?

When she came out of hospital a few days later (they wanted to keep her in to check that she was stable enough to be safe) I had to talk to her about it – but how do you broach a subject like that? Luckily, now her secret was out, she seemed willing to talk. I gave her a big hug when I saw her, and she apologised for scaring me, and said there was nothing I could have done, then explained that she'd been struggling with depression for years, because she'd had a traumatic childhood. Now she was on antidepressants – after her overdose, the doctors insisted on it – but she'd been on them before and didn't think that they worked.

The next fortnight was hell. She was up and down all the time: sometimes unable to get out of bed for a day and a half, and at others calling me at midnight suggesting we went clubbing. Keeping up with her roller-coaster moods was hard work, but I had to be there for her – she was my friend. Then she seemed to settle down. After about six months on the pills,

In It for the Long Haul

she wasn't getting tearful as much, and didn't seem to be so exuberant either. It wasn't a bad change though - she was just 'one of the gang' rather than the centre of attention now.

But then she decided to come off the pills. Within a week, she was back to her old self, and, sadly, she attempted suicide again. Luckily, a friend found her and got her to hospital in time to get her stomach pumped but it was terrifying anyway. She said afterwards that it wasn't a cry for help - she just didn't want to exist any more because it hurt too much. I encouraged her to go back to the doctors and, although it took her over a month, eventually she did. She went back onto the pills and agreed she'd only come off them under the doctor's instruction - and gradually, rather than just stopping overnight (apparently, that was why her side-effects had been so bad).

Since then, there have been good times and bad. I know that she'll sometimes cancel things we've arranged at the last minute because she feels too depressed to leave the house, or simply can't - agoraphobia is one of her symptoms. And I know that I have to be careful around subjects that trigger her moods: usually men or anything that she's not in control of. But she's a brilliant friend: she gives as much as she takes. Whenever I'm going through a hard time, she's there for me, and will patiently listen for hours. She's explained a lot about the way her illness works to me as well, so I've learned about depression through her. She says it's like any other illness, and, much as I wouldn't dump a mate for getting cancer, I'm not going to leave her in the lurch just because sometimes she gets depressed.

You Must Be My Best Friend ...

DOMESTIC VIOLENCE: A SCARY REALITY

A quarter of women and one in six men suffer from domestic violence at some stage in their life, so, given that most of us have six true friends over the course of our lives, it's statistically likely that you'll encounter a friend who's either being abused by a partner, or has been in the past. You might think it could never happen to anyone you know, but domestic violence can happen to anyone, of any age, from any class. Just because someone is educated, well dressed or charming in public, it doesn't mean that they can't be an abuser.

If you find out that a friend is suffering from domestic violence, your automatic reaction will probably be to urge them to leave. If they don't, you may find it hard to understand why they put up with the behaviour, and assume they're weak or to blame for what's happening, but the issue is much more complex than that.

While every couple has arguments to a lesser or greater degree, in a balanced relationship both partners are able to retain their own personality, state their opinions and make their own decisions without any fear.

In an abusive relationship, this isn't the case. Instead, one partner tries to control the relationship through imposing their will on the other. This can take the form of criticism, unacceptable demands, threats or physical violence – and all of these can be equally damaging. Sex can also be used as a control mechanism, with one partner insisting on getting sex their way, on their terms, with no thought to the other's happiness or willingness to comply. Often, people try to excuse an abusive partner's behaviour by blaming it on drink, drugs, stress, or even on their own actions. This is wrong: abuse is never acceptable, regardless of the situation, and is never the victim's fault. It happens because the abuser wants to manipulate and control their partner. But it can be hard to spot this when you're in an abusive relationship.

Because of the way that an abuser demeans his partner, your friend may feel too insecure to share her problem with you directly. However, if you get a bad vibe and think that something's going on, watch for certain behaviours; she may mention that her other half is possessive, jealous or bad-tempered. If your friend seems to be scared of her partner, or is constantly anxious to please him, there could be an issue — particularly if he also criticises or humiliates her in front of other people. And if he makes all the decisions — financial, social or otherwise — then it can also indicate problems. Similarly, if you talk about sex and she says she's pressured to do things that she doesn't want to then this should also set off warning bells.

Another common occurrence when someone's being abused is that they're banned from seeing friends and family, or even refused *any* access to them, so if your friend has to cut phone conversations short when her partner's around, it could indicate a problem. And if she has become quieter, lost

You Must Be My Best Friend ...

her confidence or is more anxious or depressed then this can also be a sign that things aren't as they should be.

Obviously, if your friend has unexplained physical injuries, or brushes off any questions with an unfeasible excuse ('I walked into a door'), then you should be on your guard. And if your friend splits up with a partner who then constantly calls her, harasses her, visits her or stalks her, it could suggest there's more to the breakup than just a row.

If you spot any signs that make you think a friend is being abused, be supportive rather than critical about her staying in the situation. If someone who's being abused feels like they're being judged or criticised, it can make them clam up and refuse to share what's happening to them with anyone else, as well as stay in the situation. And as domestic violence tends to start with the abuser demeaning their partner and damaging their confidence, adding to the criticism will only make things worse.

Added to that, there are many reasons people stay in a situation where they're being abused, and you may not know the whole story; your friend might be scared her partner will get more violent, or harm her friends or family if she leaves. Her abuser may have threatened to kill himself if she dumps him; or she may still love him — at least when he's not abusing her. Some people's religious beliefs stop them from leaving a violent partner, and many people who are abused believe that their partner will change, given enough time. There's also the problem that people who are abused tend to blame themselves for what's happening.

In It for the Long Haul

Because of the myriad reasons that people have for staying in an abusive relationship, it's essential that you don't make your friend feel there's something wrong with her if she wants to stay. This will only reinforce her guilt, low confidence and view that it's all her fault.

Added to this, it can be dangerous leaving an abusive partner as the violence may escalate. The best you can do as a friend is help her to think about things, decide how she feels and what she can do, and help her consider her safety whether she decides to stay with her partner or not. Don't judge her; respect her decisions and help her protect herself both emotionally and physically. You can also give her details of domestic violence support services (see Useful Resources).

You might be embarrassed about tackling the issue, but if you approach a friend in a non-critical and sensitive way, she's more than likely to be grateful for the concern, even if she doesn't want to talk about the situation (or you're suspicions are wrong). To initiate the conversation, start by explaining that you're concerned about her and then explain why – for example, say: 'I'm worried that you seem much less confident nowadays.' Your pal may well go on the defensive but don't be put off – it could be that she's having a hard time trusting anyone after what's happened to her at the hands of someone 'who loves her', or she may not be ready to talk about it. And if your friend is male, it can be even harder for him to admit he's being abused, fearing that it shows he's unmanly or weak.

You Must Be My Best Friend ...

It won't necessarily be easy to help a friend who's in a domestic violence situation: they may deny what's going on or reject your support. Don't push matters if that's the case – just say you're there if they ever need you. Be patient and look for any clues that they're ready to talk about the abuse.

If your friend does talk to you about the abuse, make sure that you say you believe her and take what she says seriously. People are much more likely to downplay abuse than exaggerate it. While it might be hard for you to believe, particularly if you think you know her partner well, it's impossible to know what goes on behind closed doors, and she could be in real danger.

Reassure her after she's told you about the abuse, letting her know how brave you think she is, and generally compliment her as much as you can. By rebuilding her confidence, you'll help her get the strength to deal with what she's going through – and hopefully come out the other side. And let her know the abuse isn't her fault and that no one has the right to abuse another person.

Talk to your friend about ways to look after herself: encourage her to think of what she can do and how you can help her achieve it. Don't give her advice – she has to make the decision for herself and by deciding for her, you'll reduce her confidence in her ability to deal with things herself. Instead, ask questions like: 'What can I do to help you?', 'How does he make you feel?' or, 'What are you afraid of if you leave him?' – without a judgemental tone.

In It for the Long Haul

Avoid asking, 'Why do you put up with it?' or, 'How can you love someone who hits you?' as these imply it's your friend's fault. And don't try to work out the reasons for the abuse: they're irrelevant because there is no excuse for it. That said, don't criticise her partner as it may make her withdraw. Instead, criticise his *behaviour*. The last thing you want is her springing to his defence.

It's worth bearing in mind that practical support like offering her a car or a place to stay can be just as useful as emotional support. If your friend is willing, help her prepare an emergency bag, with money, her keys, some clothes, her bank cards, driver's licence, property deeds, medication, birth certificates, passport and any other important documents. You can always store it for her if she's scared of it being discovered. You can also offer to be a witness, in case she ever wants to prosecute. If you feel able to offer this, take notes when you observe abuse, with the times, dates, and what you saw – or even better, capture it on film or a camera phone if you can do so without risking your own safety.

Staying in regular contact can also help your friend get through things. You may want to devise a code word she can use if things get really bad, so that you know what's going on, or help her come up with convincing excuses she can use to her abuser if she needs to leave.

And remember to keep regular contact up even if she does leave him, as that can sometimes be the hardest time. Make sure she's aware of how the police can help her, with Intervention Orders or even a panic button depending on the situation.

Remember, leaving a domestically violent situation is your

friend's decision to make, not yours; while abuse is never acceptable, you need to respect her right to make her own decisions based on her own beliefs and culture.

Both sides of the story

If you know the person who's abusing your friend, you may feel like you're trapped between them, and need to approach the abuser. If you witness the abuse, and you think it's safe to tackle the subject, then talk about what you've seen. For example, say, 'You know I'm friends with both of you, but I think the way you criticise and intimidate her is wrong.' However, if you only know about the abuse because your friend has told you she's being abused, check with her first before raising the subject. The abuser might get more violent if he thinks she's told someone.

Even if you do talk to the abuser, they could lie, tell you to mind your own business, downplay what's happened, blame it on their partner or say that they couldn't help it because they were drunk or out of control. None of these responses mean that there isn't domestic violence happening – a lot of abusers deny what they're doing. And if they do admit it, they won't necessarily know how to stop their behaviour, so give them support and encourage them to seek professional help. Sometimes, a man will find it easier to speak to another man about the problem, and a woman will find it easier to speak to another woman, so encourage them towards support groups. Don't try to 'solve the problem' or analyse why someone is abusive — it will help them excuse what they're doing. Instead, focus on what the person who is abusive is going to do about it, and encourage them to seek professional help.

Help yourself too

Supporting a friend who's being abused can be hard for you too, so make sure that you get support. Obviously, it's not the kind of thing that you should chat about with friends at random, but it's worth confiding in at least one friend, or a support service, so that you don't feel you're tackling it on your own. It's important that your friend can't see your frustration or disappointment if she doesn't leave her partner because otherwise it can feed back into her lack of self-worth. As such, you need to offload it somewhere.

It's also worth being aware of your own safety. Don't put yourself at risk by trying to get involved in the situation with her partner directly; not only could they hurt you but they could also manipulate you. If you see your friend being abused, call the police instead of wading in.

Don't underestimate how important what you're doing is. Whether your partner stays in the abusive relationship or not, by being there for her, you're doing the most that a friend can. If it starts to get too much for you, don't feel bad about taking a break from helping. You can only support your friend if you make sure you're in a fit state to do it. And, harsh as it sounds, it's not your job to rescue your friend. Only she can save herself.

You Must Be My Best Friend ...

Jennifer's story: She hit him

My friend Peter is a really nice bloke: intelligent, funny and creative. He's also a martial arts expert. So when he told me one night that his new girlfriend was hitting him, at first I thought he must be joking. I mean, he's well over six foot, and she's under five feet tall. Surely he could defend himself against her? He'd mentioned it in a jokey way – 'Better get back, don't want Marsha to get mad and lay into me,' – so I just thought that it was his sense of humour.

I didn't see Peter for a while after that – about a month. We normally see each other most weeks but I figured that it was just first rush of lust and left it at that. But when I next saw him, I thought something was wrong. He was quieter than normal, and made a lot more self-deprecating comments. He seemed to apologise for everything he did – accidentally spilling a drop of beer when he carried a round over; tapping his feet when a song he liked came on. He wasn't like the lairy Peter I knew and loved. I asked if he was OK and he said that he was. I thought that he might have said something more, but Marsha turned up and they left soon afterwards.

It was over a month until I next saw him – and this time, I was genuinely worried. He had a black eye – something utterly out of character. He abhors violence – his martial arts training gave him that – and when he said he'd tripped and fell, without giving any more details, I remembered what he'd said about Marsha when they first started seeing each other. The only way

In It for the Long Haul

I could think to bring it up was through humour. 'As long as Marsha's not beating you,' I joked. He looked at me and I realised that she was.

Luckily, Marsha had got a hen weekend with her best mate a few days later, so Peter and I had time to talk. Apparently, she was fine until she'd had a drink but then she got really possessive. She'd wait behind the door for him with a frying pan, or even pour boiling tea over him. I couldn't help crying when he told me what he'd been through. She also told him it was his own fault - he drove her to it by being so flirtatious and having female friends. I helped him see that this wasn't the case - he was the same lovely Peter as always. When she came back, I was with him (at his request) and he told her he wanted them to split up. She shouted and screamed at him, calling him worthless and criticising his sexual technique, but I held his hand when things got bad (that got a whole load more abuse, aimed at 'the slag' - me) and we walked away from her ranting.

It took Peter a long time to trust any woman enough to be his girlfriend again, but now he's with a lovely woman, Pamela, and his confidence is back to normal. It showed me that anyone can get attacked by a partner though - it's not as obvious as you might think.

* * *

You Must Be My Best Friend ...

Like it or not, sometimes, the only solution to a friend's problems is to leave them to it to work it out themselves. If you've been bashing your head against a brick wall, trying to encourage your friend to get out of a bad relationship, give up a drug habit or deal with mental health issues, and they're still not doing anything about it, tough love can be the only answer. If a friendship makes you feel bad about yourself, or gets you into negative behaviours, then you may have to cut and run. It doesn't make you a bad friend; but everyone is responsible for their own happiness, and if a friend makes you sad all the time, she's not someone it's good to have in your life. For your own sake, and hers, you should bail.

Of course, it's not just addiction, depression or domestic violence that can put a strain on your relationship. Serious or terminal illness, rape, or the death of a loved one can all have almost as much of an impact on you as on a friend who's suffering. The best course of action with all of these is to offer support, be there for your friend and make sure you listen. Let your friend know that they are loved and that they have no reason to feel guilty or as if they've done something wrong (feelings that all of the above can trigger). Ask your friend how they want to be supported and they'll tell you the best course of action.

With any luck, you'll be able to help your friend through their problem and give them the support that they need without ending up feeling lousy. And if you do manage it, one thing's guaranteed: your friendship will be much stronger when you come out the other side.

In It for the Long Haul

TEN SIGNS YOU'RE IN A DAMAGING FRIENDSHIP

1. You dread meeting up with your friend and find yourself wishing you have to work late so you'd have an excuse to cancel.
2. You feel worse about yourself after seeing your friend.
3. You feel like you always end up having the same conversations about the same negative things every time you meet up.
4. You end up taking part in negative behaviours – drinking or taking drugs to excess whenever you're with each other.
5. You've thought about stopping seeing her but can't because you're too scared of her.
6. She only wants to see you when you're giving her something, be it free tickets to the cinema, a birthday present or a listening ear.
7. If you have a problem, your friend won't listen, but if she has one, she expects you to drop everything.
8. She can remember every tiny slight and negative comment you've ever made about her – most of which she's imagined – and reminds you about them on a regular basis.
9. You're scared to show her your latest purchases or talk about your life because you know she'll try to copy it.
10. Your other friends keep asking you what it is that you see in her because she treats you so badly.

Conclusion

Friends till the End

By now, friendship may be seeming like more hassle than it's worth, what with all the insecurity, rows and general risks to your sanity. But don't give up on it. After all, people say that friends are the new family, and think about how many rows you've had with your family over the years.

If you've got a healthy friendship (or six) then you've got someone who you can confide your darkest secrets to, without panicking you'll get judged or have your confidence breached. You've got someone who you can socialise with, who'll hold your hair back when you're throwing up after one too many tequilas. A friend will warn you when beer goggles are the only thing that's making you think you're chatting to Mr Right when, in fact, he's the Elephant Man's brother – and the Elephant Man was the one that got the looks. They'll help you feel happier when you're sad, build your confidence back up when you get dumped, and can be useful for doing the 'my friend fancies you' thing (if you're not too terrified of coming across as a cliché).

You Must Be My Best Friend ...

If you've got a friend, you'll never go through life truly alone; partners may come and go but a good friendship can last you for life. Of course, the downside is that your friend will remember all those partners who have been and gone, so can tease you mercilessly about that time you dated that 'creative' bloke who turned out to be an unemployed work-shy drug-dealing idiot, whose sole creative act was scrawling unintelligible lyrics on the back of beer mats when he was wasted. But hey, having someone who can remind you about the mistakes you've made is handy when it comes to avoiding making the same mistakes again.

Sorry seems to be the hardest word

While most of this book has been about dealing with friends who turn into nightmares, it's fair to say that sometimes you'll be the one who messes up. From accidental things, like borrowing your friend's clothes/favourite book/laptop and losing or breaking it to thoughtless things like slagging off her boyfriend/children/family when you're drunk – mistakes happen. Lovely as it would be to be blameless and consistently right, at times we all mess up. And being prepared to apologise is essential.

Sometimes, it can be incredibly tempting to lie – particularly if your friend doesn't know about the mistake you've made. While this may seem like the easy route, imagine the guilt when your friend comes to you in tears about what's happened, or rants to you about the idiot who broke her computer then sneaked away without telling her. So stop being pathetic. Front up, offer to pay if you've damaged something and grovel.

If your friend knows that you've made a mistake — say, you spent a night telling her how rubbish her boyfriend is courtesy of too many glasses of wine — deal with the problem sooner rather than later. The longer you wait, the more she'll get to stew about what you've done. Don't lie and say that you didn't mean it — that will only lead to the argument inflating when she asks why you did it. Instead, say, 'Sorry I said what I said last night. I spoke out of turn and it was inappropriate. I didn't mean to hurt you,' or similar. It might take her a while to get over it, but at least by apologising, you're trying to rectify things.

If you've had a major row with a friend and she won't accept your calls or agree to meet you, drop her an email or send her a letter instead. If you really messed up, you might want to consider chucking a bunch of flowers into the mix too — after all, it works for men who make mistakes!

Apologies should never be given grudgingly or with a caveat — 'Sorry I ripped your dress but I told you it was too small for me,' — but instead should be genuine. Don't expect instant forgiveness — it may take your friend a little while to lick her wounds — but if she still hasn't forgiven you in a month or so, she's holding a grudge for far too long. Unless, of course, you slept with her boyfriend, got her fired or stole her dog and sold it to a furrier, in which case you'll probably never get her to forgive you.

You Must Be My Best Friend ...

AND FINALLY ...

As with any relationship, friendship takes work and is likely to go through ebbs and flows. But by putting in the effort – even if all that sometimes entails is being prepared to take a back seat in your friend's life for a while – you'll develop much healthier friendships and feel better in yourself. To go all 'Hallmark' on you, the best way to have good friends is to *be* a good friend. Treat other people as you'd like to be treated and you won't go far wrong. Unless, of course, your friend turns out to be a nightmare bitch from hell. But look on the bright side: even if she is, you'll have good anecdotes to tell your friends in years to come.

TEN REASONS THAT FRIENDS ARE WORTH THE EFFORT – EVEN IF YOU DO HATE THEM AT TIMES

1. They can tell you when you're getting into bad habits, be that dating awful men or making career mistakes – and respect you enough to let you make those mistakes again if you think it's the right thing to do.
2. You have someone to share your successes with, who'll be proud of you.
3. The more friends you have, the bigger your collective wardrobe/book collection/amount of floors to crash on.

Friends till the End

4. You've always got someone to sound out about your latest partner; and friends can judge much more objectively than you can, because they're not wearing rose-tinted glasses.
5. They can tell you when you're being neurotic/over-analytical/panicking over nothing, and, unlike a partner saying it, you're likely to listen to them.
6. They'll tell you honestly but tactfully if you look lousy in your favourite dress.
7. You can have fun with them – and fun is an essential part of life.
8. They love you. Being loved is a great ego-boost, as well as being good for your self-esteem.
9. They know all your secrets – and you wouldn't want them getting out now, would you?
10. No matter how much they might annoy you at times, a good friendship will give you a warm glow inside – even if you wouldn't admit it for fear of sounding overly sentimental.

Useful Resources

Dealing with depression

The Samaritans
UK: 08457 90 90 90 (24 hours)
Ireland: 1850 60 90 90 (24 hours)
www.samaritans.org.uk
The Samaritans provide confidential emotional support for people who are experiencing feelings of distress or despair, including those that may lead to suicide.

Dealing with an addict

Al-Anon Family Groups UK and Eire
020 7403 0888
www.alcoholics-anonymous.org
Support group for friends, family and partners of alcoholics.

Helping a friend cope with domestic violence

National Domestic Violence Helpline
0808 200 0247 (24 hours)
UK-based national helpline providing access to advice and support to anyone experiencing domestic violence.

You Must Be My Best Friend ...

Women's Aid
0808 200 0247 (24 hours)

www.womensaid.org.uk

Domestic violence helpline. Women's Aid can also give details of refuges and the availability of refuge places throughout the UK.

Scottish Domestic Abuse Helpline
0800 027 1234 (24 hours)

www.domesticabuse.co.uk

Domestic abuse helpline, providing housing, legal and benefits advice for all parts of Scotland.

Refuge
0808 200 0247 (24 hours)

www.refuge.org.uk

Provides safe, emergency accommodation through a network of refuges throughout the UK.

Everyman Project
020 7263 8884 (Tuesday and Wednesday, 6.30pm – 9pm)

www.everymanproject.co.uk.

Offers counselling to men in the London area who want to change their violent or abusive behaviour, and a national helpline offering advice to anyone worried about their own, or someone else's, violent or abusive behaviour.

M-Power
0808 808 4321 (Thursday evenings only, 8pm – 10pm)

www.male-rape.org.uk

A national helpline for men who have who have been raped, assaulted or abused in childhood or adult life. The helpline also supports partners (male and female) and family members of abused men.

About the Author

Emily Dubberley (31) is a writer and editor on the subjects of relationships and sex. She is editor-at-large, and was the founding editor, of Scarlet — a national women's magazine combining a feisty no-bullshit attitude to life with erotic fiction — and her books include *Brief Encounters: The Women's Guide to Casual Sex*, *Things a Woman Should Know About Seduction*, *Sex Play* and *The Lovers' Guide Lovemaking Deck*. She was shortlisted for the Company Prize for Fiction, the *Cosmopolitan* Journalism Scholarship, campaigner of the year in the Erotic Awards 2003 and writer of the year in the Erotic Awards 2005.

Her other projects include creating www.cliterati.co.uk and www.bibibaby.com, writing three *Lovers' Guide* videos: *Sex Positions*, *Sex Play* and *7 Secrets to a Passionate Love Life*, editing the *Lovers' Guide* magazine and co-founding www.loversguide.com.

Despite her apparent obsession with sex, she thinks that friends are much more important than getting laid. Unless it's with someone really hot, of course.

Brief Encounters
The Women's Guide to Casual Sex
Emily Dubberley

You don't need to be in a relationship to have sex, and this ultimate guide to no-strings sex ensures that single doesn't have to mean celibate. From pulling your ultimate lust object to getting rid of them the next morning, sex writer Emily Dubberley tells you everything you need to know to have good casual sex.

Find out how to cope with lousy kissers, miniscule (and massive) members and the nightmare of working out someone's name the next day. Incredibly useful and lots of fun, *Brief Encounters* is the essential guide to having the ride(s) of your life.

'Feisty, funny and spot on!'
Dr. Pam Spurr, author of
The Dating Survival Guide

'Fascinating, informative, amusing and scary as hell. This book is full of advice aimed at giving women an unfair advantage.'
Mil Millington, author of
Things my Girlfriend and I have Argued About

Non-fiction: Sex/Relationships
1-904132-66-9
£10.99
$17.95

Chilfree and Loving It!

Nicki Defago

'The responsibility of parenthood is overwhelming and incredibly stressful. And it's for life. Don't give up a pleasant life, for a life of unpaid drudgery. Your standard of living drastically declines, and the kids take off as soon as they can, without a backward glance.'
Shirley Conran

We live in a child-centred society. Women, no matter how high achieving in other areas, are pitied and patronised if they are childless, and condemned as selfish if this is by choice. However large numbers of women are enjoying their hard-won independence, and are reluctant to give it all up to become slaves to their children. And many men feel the same way.

Childfree and Loving It! is a broad, definitive exploration of non-parenthood, challenging the myths of parenthood and boldly proclaiming the joys of a childfree life. Nicki Defago explores population growth and the environment, workplace policies and consumerism, and interviews those who have chosen not to have children as well as the honest parents who wish they hadn't.

If you have ever questioned the need for children or sighed with relief that you don't have any – then this is the book for you.

Non-fiction: Sociology/Parenting
1-904132-63-4
£10.99
$17.95